Peak District
Mountain Biking
Dark Peak Trails

VERTEBRATE PUBLISHING

Design and production by Vertebrate Publishing, Sheffield
www.v-publishing.co.uk

Peak District
MountainBiking
Dark Peak Trails

Written by
Jon Barton

Photography by **John Coefield**

Peak District
MountainBiking
Dark Peak Trails

Front cover photo: Cy Turner on Whinstone Lee Tor singletrack, above Ladybower Reservoir.
Back cover photo: Jon Barton and Tom Fenton begin the drop into Stanage Plantation.

Photography by **John Coefield, unless otherwise credited.**

 All maps reproduced by permission of Ordnance Survey
on behalf of The Controller of Her Majesty's Stationery Office.
© Crown Copyright. 100025218

 Design by Nathan Ryder, production by Jane Beagley.
www.**v-graphics**.co.uk

VERTEBRATE **GRAPHICS**

 Mixed Sources
Product group from well-managed forests
and other controlled sources
www.fsc.org   Cert no. DNV-COC-000087
©1996 Forest Stewardship Council

Contents

ROUTE GRADES
▲ = MEDIUM ▲ = HARD ▲ = EXTREME (see page ix)

THE AUTHOR UP ON CHINLEY CHURN, KINDER IN THE DISTANCE

Introduction

There's no doubting the Dark Peak offers excellent riding – some of the best in the world. The Peak District is criss-crossed with ancient roads, moorland trails and technical open ground; it has been a worthy challenge reriding, checking and collating the rides in this book. Rest assured, the routes feature a fierce collection of climbs, some very challenging descents and some sublime stretches of open trail, swooping across this rugged landscape.

In an update over the first edition, all the routes in this book are taken from the area of the Peak District covered by the Ordnance Survey OL1 The Dark Peak map – well, apart from a couple of hundred metres on Blacka Moor that nip south onto the White Peak sheet! The Dark Peak is an area that gives us real mountain biking: these rides are hard, exhausting and they will destroy bikes and components. Yet they are equally rewarding, offering a wealth of experiences – some of my happiest moments on a bike have been spent high on the Howden Moors, or traversing Win Hill.

Contained in these pages are many routes and clues of what to expect and how best to enjoy the area. They will take you to the brink of world-class downhills, carry you across ribbons of moorland singletrack and challenge you on some real climbs. Cave Dale, Cut Gate, Whinstone Lee Tor, Jaggers Clough, Middle Moor...what pleasures we have on these legendary trails. Stop every now and again and enjoy the landscape; it truly is beautiful, the wildlife, people and spirit of the place is quite special, I know you will respect it, and keep coming back for more.

This book builds on that guidebook, the guidebook that changed the way mountain bikers produced and used guides, *Dark Peak Mountain Biking – True Grit Trails*. Of course I have carried forward many classics from that volume, some have been refined a little as we found better ways and new delights to ride, quite a few are longer – but I know you wanted that. I have added a few new rides and lost a few abused ones. I've also dragged the photographer over every inch of the Dark Peak in order to serve up the finest selection of inspirational images we could produce – although to be fair he loved every minute of it.

Thanks to everyone who supported our first guide to the Dark Peak, it gives me a real buzz when I see someone leaning on a gate, out there on the true grit trails reading about the next leg of their ride. Give us a nod as you ride by.

Jon Barton

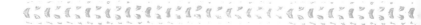

Acknowledgements

First of all, thanks to the many, many thousands of riders out there who supported *Dark Peak Mountain Biking – True Grit Trails*, and its companion volume *White Peak Mountain Biking*. It really means a lot to have worked on these books and to have seen so many people use them.

Thanks to everyone at Vertebrate Graphics and Vertebrate Publishing; this book has an amazing editor in John Coefield, and the routes are brought to life like no other previous MTB guidebook by John's stunning photography. Thanks also to Tim Russon for his excellent additional images and for being a willing model in the pictures he and his wife Kim feature in. Thanks must also go to our other models; Tom Fenton, Cy Turner, Catherine Bowman and Matt Withycombe. Thanks also to Teija, Nathan, Jane and Simon at Vertebrate who also in their own skilled and professional way helped to see this project come to life.

Thanks to Cy at Cotic (the Hemlock is awesome!), to Si and Matt at 18bikes for advice, servicing and putting up with me milling around the second best bike shop in the UK. Also thanks to Sealskinz and Gore for riding kit, and to Nikki at Rab for inadvertently supplying riding jackets! Thanks to Judith at the Woodbine for the cups of tea. Thanks to Mike Rhodes at the National Park and Geoff Lomas at Yorkshire Water for route and access advice. Many people have offered advice on route choice, and helped test rides; big you all up. Thanks to Paul Evans for the inspiration from our first volume together. And of course my lovely wife Gráinne and son Thomas, my future cycling buddy.

How to Use This Book

The Routes

This guide contains what I consider the best routes in the Dark Peak (in my humble opinion) – arguably one of the best places to ride a mountain bike in the UK. The aim with the routes is to showcase what's on offer and encourage you to ride in new areas, to try new trails and to get to know and love the area as I do. Try the routes as suggested, ride some in reverse (debates will rage about which way some trails should be ridden for years to come) and link rides together with neighbouring rides. That's the great thing with mountain biking, as long as we stay on the trails we're allowed on (i.e. not footpaths) then there are pretty much no rules – how good is that!

Roughly speaking, **Classics** are generally fairly short (although not necessarily easy), **Epics** are a little longer and climb a little more. **Enduros** are a step up again, and the **Killers** are pretty self-explanatory. We've also chucked in some other handy stuff, such as A to B rides, links out from Sheffield and top tens.

Grades

Routes, climbs and descents are graded blue, red and black, in a similar system to that used at trail centres around the UK.

▲ = Easy ▲ = Moderate ▲ = Hard

Blue graded routes are generally shorter routes and are within reach of most MTBers, even newcomers, as well as the kind of thing you could do in a short day or when the weather's really foul. **Reds** are the kind of rides that won't actually take a full day, but you'll probably not want to do anything else once you've ridden them. And **Blacks** are those big and memorable days out that will demand endurance and some technical ability in places. These are the kind of routes to work up to.

The grades are based on average conditions – good weather and not too wet and muddy. In a drought the routes will feel easier, in the depths of winter, harder. Grades consider technicality, length, climbs, navigation, and remoteness – so one 'black' route might be a short all-out technical test while another could be a big endurance challenge with tricky navigation. As ever, these grades are subjective. How you find a particular route, downhill or climb will be dictated by your own levels of fitness and skill.

Directions & Accuracy

While every effort has been made to ensure accuracy within the directions in this guide, things change and we are unable to guarantee that every detail will be correct. Please treat stated distances as guidelines. **Please exercise caution if a direction appears at odds with the route on the ground. A comparison between direction and map should see you on the right track.**

Rights of Way

Countryside access in the UK hasn't been particularly kind to cyclists, although things are improving. We have 'right of way' on bridleways (blue arrows on signs) and byways (red arrows). However, having 'right of way' doesn't actually mean having the right of way, just that we're allowed to ride there – so give way to walkers and horse riders. We're also allowed to ride on green lanes and some unclassified roads, although the only way to determine which are legal and which aren't is to check with the local authority. Obviously, cycle routes are also in.

Everything else is out of bounds (unless, of course, the landowner says otherwise). Riding illegally can upset walkers (who have every right to enjoy their day) and is, in many cases, technically classed as trespass (meaning you could be prosecuted for any damage caused). Not all tracks are signed, so it's not always obvious whether that great-looking trail you want to follow is an illegal footpath or a legal bridleway. That's why it's a good idea to carry a map with you on every ride.

The Bike

Any half-decent mountain bike will be fine (try and avoid a '£99 special'). A full suspension bike will add comfort and control. A lightweight race number will make hills easier and something with a bit of travel will help on technical descents. We'd pick a compromise somewhere between the three, depending on your personal preferences.

Check everything's working – you won't be going uphill fast if your gears seize but equally you'll be a little quicker than planned if your brakes fail coming down. Pump the tyres up, check nothing's about to wear through and make sure that everything that should be tight is tight.

Essential Kit

Helmet

"The best helmet is the one that you're wearing". Make sure it fits, you're wearing it correctly and that it won't move in a crash.

Clothing

You need to get your clothing right if you want to stay comfortable on a bike, especially in bad weather. The easiest way to do this is to follow a layering system. Begin with clothing made from 'technical' synthetic or wool fabrics that will wick the sweat away from your

body and then dry quickly, keeping you dry and warm. Stay away from cotton – it absorbs moisture and holds onto it. If it's chilly, an insulating layer will keep you warm, and a wind/waterproof layer on the outside protects from the elements. Layers can then be removed or added to suit the conditions. Padded shorts are more comfortable, but the amount of lycra on display is down to you. Baggy shorts, full length tights and trousers are all available to match the conditions. Set off a little on the cold side – you'll soon warm up. Don't leave the warm clothes behind though, as the weather can turn quickly.

Gloves
Gloves ward off blisters and numb hands and help keep your fingers warm. They also provide a surprising amount of protection when you come off.

Footwear
Flat pedals/clips-ins – it's your call. Make sure you can walk in the shoes and that they have sufficient tread for you to do so. Consider overshoes if it's chilly.

Other essentials
As mentioned, take any necessary spares, tools, tube and pump, spare clothes, first aid kit, food and water. Stop short of the kitchen sink, as you'll still want to be able to actually ride your bike.

You'll need something to carry this lot in. We'd suggest a hydration pack, as they allow you to drink on the move and keep excess weight off the bike.

General Safety
The ability to read a map, navigate in poor visibility and to understand weather warnings is essential. Don't head out in bad weather, unless you're confident and capable of doing so.

Some of the routes described point you at tough climbs and steep descents that can potentially be very dangerous. Too much exuberance on a steep descent in the middle of nowhere and you could be in more than a spot of bother, especially if you're alone. Consider your limitations and relative fragility.

Be self-sufficient. Carry food and water, spares, a tube and a pump. Consider a first aid kit. Even if it's warm, the weather could turn, so take a wind/waterproof. Think about what could happen on an enforced stop. Pack lights if you could finish in the dark.

If you're riding solo, think about the seriousness of an accident – you might be without help for a very long time. Tell someone where you're going, when you'll be back and tell them once you are back. Take a mobile phone if you have one, but don't expect a signal. And **don't** call out the ambulance because you've grazed your knee.

Riding in a group is safer (ambitious overtaking manoeuvres excepted) and often more fun, but don't leave slower riders too far behind and give them a minute for a breather when they've caught up. Allow extra time for a group ride, as you'll inevitably stop and chat. You might need an extra top if you're standing around for a while. Ride within your ability, make sure you can slow down fast and give way to other users. Bells might be annoying, but they work. If you can't bring yourself to bolt one on, a polite 'excuse me' should be fine. **On hot, sunny days, slap on some Factor 30+ and** ALWAYS WEAR YOUR HELMET!

In the Event of an Accident

In the event of an accident requiring immediate assistance: Dial 999 and ask for POLICE or AMBULANCE. If you can supply the services with a grid reference of exactly where you are it should help to speed up their response time.

Rules of the (Off) Road

1. Always ride on legal trails.
2. Ride considerately – give way to horses and pedestrians.
3. Don't spook animals.
4. Ride in control – you don't know who's around the next corner.
5. Leave gates as you find them – if you're unsure, shut them.
6. Keep the noise down and don't swear loudly when you fall off in front of walkers.
7. Leave no trace – take home everything you took out.
8. Keep water sources clean – don't take toilet stops near streams.
9. Enjoy the countryside and respect its life and work.

Planning Your Ride

1. Consider the ability/experience of each rider in your group. Check the weather forecast. How much time do you have available? Now choose your route.
2. Study the route description before setting off, and cross-reference it with the relevant map.
3. Bear in mind everything we've suggested about safety, clothing, spares and food and drink.
4. Get out there and get dirty.

Maps & Symbols

Ordnance Survey maps are the most commonly used, are easy to read and many people are happy using them. If you're not familiar with OS maps and are unsure of what the symbols mean, you can download a free map legend from **www.v-outdoor.co.uk**

Here's a guide to the symbols and abbreviations we use on the maps and in our directions:

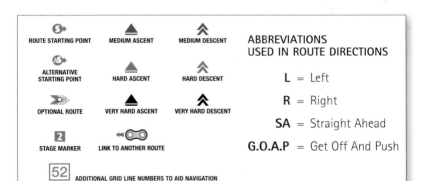

ROUTE STARTING POINT

ALTERNATIVE STARTING POINT

OPTIONAL ROUTE

STAGE MARKER

52 ADDITIONAL GRID LINE NUMBERS TO AID NAVIGATION

MEDIUM ASCENT

HARD ASCENT

VERY HARD ASCENT

LINK TO ANOTHER ROUTE

MEDIUM DESCENT

HARD DESCENT

VERY HARD DESCENT

ABBREVIATIONS USED IN ROUTE DIRECTIONS

L = Left

R = Right

SA = Straight Ahead

G.O.A.P = Get Off And Push

Peak District
Mountain**Biking**
Area Map & Route Finder

SECTION 1

Classics

A quick blast after work, a night loop you can finish before your lights die, or a ride to squeeze in when time is short. That's a classic. Relatively low on distance, short, but not necessarily easy, these are still good, solid rides.

Classics
sponsored by **GORE**
BIKE WEAR™

ANCIENT TRAILS OVER HOUNDKIRK MOOR (ROUTE 1)

TIM RUSSON ON WIMBLE HOLME HILL SINGLETRACK

01 Blacka Moor – East Peak

16.5km

Introduction

Sitting tight against the eastern boundary of the Peak District National Park, and only a few short miles from Sheffield, the trails on Blacka Moor are popular with locals who ride them often as quick evening blasts (even in winter – get your lights out!). It's no exaggeration when we say there's about a zillion ways of linking the trails on Blacka Moor, Totley Moor and Houndkirk Moor. Some trails lend themselves to being ridden in either direction, while some are very much a one-way affair, such as our preferred drop through Blacka Plantation.

Making the most of the fine riding in the area, this loop is a bona fide Peak District classic. Enjoy!

The Ride

Kicking off from the Norfolk Arms, halfway up Ringinglow Road (be glad you're not a city resident and had to cycle up it), a short warm-up on tarmac leads to the byway over Houndkirk Moor. A classic wide, yet interesting, sandstone track, this leads across the moor, with expansive views from the summit towards the Derwent Valley and Kinder Plateau. Brief road work leads to a bridleway and track on Totley Moor and a fine piece of hidden narrow singletrack that contours around Wimble Holme Hill. A quick climb leads back to the road and then the highlight of the route – the drop down the Piper Lane bridleway. Serpentine singletrack leads to technical rock work before fast singletrack through woodland spits you out on tarmac with a big grin. More climbing, first on tarmac then on rough byway leads to one last descent back to the car – ensuring you finish with a grin after a job well done.

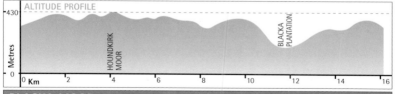

ALTITUDE PROFILE

Metres

430

0

0 Km 2 4 6 8 10 12 14 16

HOUNDKIRK MOOR

BLACKA PLANTATION

BLACKA MOOR GRADE: ▲

TOTAL DISTANCE: 16.5KM » **TOTAL ASCENT**: 450M » **TIME**: 1.5-2.5 HOURS » **START/FINISH**: LAYBY OPPOSITE NORFOLK ARMS PUB » **START GRID REF**: SK 291837 » **SATNAV**: S11 7TS » **PUB**: NORFOLK ARMS, TEL: 0114 230 2197 **CAFÉ**: NONE ON ROUTE, NEAREST LONGSHAW ESTATE

To
Miles
Tideswell - 10.
Buxton - 17.

ANCIENT RIDING ON HOUNDKIRK PHOTO: TIM RUSSON

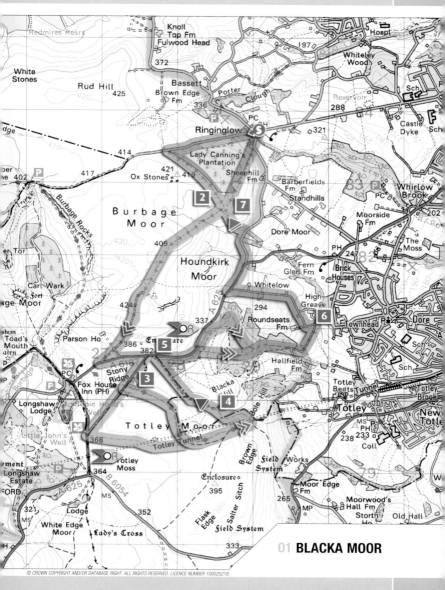

01 **BLACKA MOOR**

Directions – Blacka Moor

❺ From the car park ride up Ringinglow Road for just over 1km to a track on your left as the forest ends. Turn **L** here, signposted *Public Byway*. Follow this rough track for 1km and descend to a track crossroads.

② Turn **R** and follow the wide, rough track south-west for approx. 2.5km. Descend to a gate and turn **L** to join the A6187. Turn **L** onto this **(take care – this can be busy)**, and then **R** after 500m onto the A625.

③ Turn **L** after approx. 400m onto a signposted bridleway* and follow this as it climbs and then descends. Pass through a wooden gate/fence thing (there's actually no gate there, but it looks like there should be!) and bear **L** onto a wide, 4x4-worn track. Dodge wide, wet ruts (lakes!) for 100m at which point the track improves. Descend with increasing interest – fast then rocky – looking out for an **easy-to-miss** singletrack bridleway that bears down and **L**, approx. 50m before the first gate. Locate this (post opposite on the right) and follow it as it contours around the hillside to a gate.

*Optional Route – Wet weather option

OR In wet weather continue **SA** along the A625 and turn **L** onto a signposted bridleway just before the road junction. Rejoin the main route midway through 3. (Note this option can still be boggy in wet weather, but it tends to hold up better.).

④ Pass through the gate and bear **R** over a small wooden bridge. Continue **SA** up the field edge and turn **L** at a vague track junction in trees to climb on grass. As the track levels pass through a gate onto a rockier track and follow this to a small car park just before the main road.

⑤ Turn **R** through a small gap in the wall into the woods (footpath on map, now a Permissive Bridleway). After 500m pass through a gate and turn **R***. Drop your saddle and enjoy a brilliant descent; first singletrack, then technical, then fast. Continue **SA** at a vague path junction early on, pass through a gate, and continue **SA** as a bridleway joins from the left. Continue to eventually join tarmac and follow this to a T-junction.

*Optional Route – Devil's Elbow Descent

OB Alternatively, continue **SA** through another gate onto singletrack. Follow this to a track T-junction and turn **R** for a rootier downhill option. At a track crossroads turn **L**, signposted *Shorts Lane* and continue to the T-junction at the start of **6**.

6 Turn **L** and climb for almost 1.5km to a junction with the main road. Turn **R**, and then **L** after approx. 500m on to *Sheephill Road*. After another 400m, turn **L** through a gate on to a signposted byway, climbing back on to Houndkirk Moor.

7 Turn **R** at the track crossroads passed earlier in the route and follow this rough track to the road. Turn **L** on to this (effectively **SA**), and then **R** at Ringinglow Road to return to the start.

Making a day of it

For a longer ride that still packs in the best of Blacka, link over to Redmires and the **Stanage** Plantation descent (page 115).

VIEWS OVER SHEFFIELD FROM TOTLEY MOOR

02 Ladybower Lite

18km

Introduction

Ladybower Reservoir and its surrounding complex of hills, ridges, woodland and moorland is quite rightly a mecca for mountain bikers. This ride provides a great introduction to the area or, for return visitors, a timeless classic worthy of many a visit. Challenging, technical climbs and exhilarating descents are complemented by brilliant scenery – some of the best that Derbyshire has to offer. The paving slabs up to the twin barns remain one of the daftest, most infuriating Peak hill challenges ever.

The Ride

From Heatherdene, on the shores of Ladybower, follow the cycle path over the bridge to the foot of Crook Hill. A sharp climb past the farm leads to open pasture with fine views over to Derwent Edge on your right and Win Hill on your left. Duck into the woods and onto the fine descent of Gores Farm (Lockerbrook). A quick spin around the reservoir, past Fairholmes, leads to a tough climb up to Derwent Edge and Whinstone Lee Tor. It's worth it – the fine trail that traverses the edge, and the flying descent down to Cutthroat Bridge are world class. A final rocky tumble spits you out at the Ladybower Inn car park. Drink, anyone?

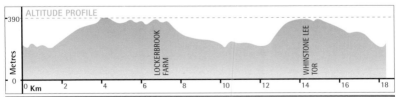

ALTITUDE PROFILE

Metres

-390

0

0 Km   2   4   6   8   10   12   14   16   18

LOCKERBROOK FARM

WHINSTONE LEE TOR

LADYBOWER LITE

GRADE: ▲

TOTAL DISTANCE: 18KM » **TOTAL ASCENT**: 700M » **TIME**: 2 HOURS » **START/FINISH**: FAIRHOLMES, LADYBOWER RESERVOIR » **START GRID REF**: SK 202859 » **SATNAV**: S33 0AZ (NEAREST) » **PUB**: LADYBOWER INN, TEL: 01433 651 241; YORKSHIRE BRIDGE INN, TEL: 01433 651 361 » **CAFÉ**: FAIRHOLMES VISITOR CENTRE, TEL: 01433 650 953

Directions — Ladybower Lite

❻ Turn **R** out of the car park, cross the road and pick up the cycle lane on the pavement near the reservoir. At the traffic lights turn **L** and continue along the cycle lane and over the bridge. Once over the bridge turn **R** up the Fairholmes/Upper Derwent Valley road.

2 Take the first **L** up steep tarmac to Crookhill Farm. Follow bridleway markers up through the farm, bearing **R** through two gates to join the track up onto Crook Hill. Follow the right-hand wall, **ignoring** all tracks that fork left. Go through a gate, follow the wall for 100m then bear **L** to cross exposed moorland, following wooden marker posts to a gate. Cross a field and go through more gates, signed *Rowlee Farm and Lockerbrook*. Go **SA** through a gate, descending with woods on the right, and **SA** through double gates ignoring a bridleway to the right. Follow a sandy/gravel track to drop down to a junction with a larger track. Turn **R** uphill to a junction with a larger track.

3 Turn **R** and drop to Lockerbrook Farm, climb a little and then start the long and ever-more thrilling descent through the trees to be spat out by the shore of Derwent Reservoir. Turn **R** and follow the tarmac road back to the mini roundabout at Fairholmes. Take the first **L** at the roundabout and drop down past Derwent Dam. Follow the road up and bear **R** at the top – effectively **SA** – to ride along the eastern shore of Ladybower Reservoir. Cross the stream at the inlet of Mill Brook and tarmac turns to hardpack. Shortly afterwards look out for a bridleway through a gate branching steeply **L** up paving slabs through a field – take this.

4 Climb up the slabs – tough at the end into the courtyard. Bear **R** through the courtyard, cross a stream and continue climbing. Continue climbing through gates, eventually emerging at the bridleway that traverses the hillside below Derwent Edge. Turn **R** and traverse the hillside to the shoulder at Whinstone Lee Tor. Savour the view then chuck yourself down the great pedally descent to Cutthroat Bridge. After almost 2km, as the path drops down and swings right towards the stream and main road, take the **R** fork to keep some height and traverse off across the moor with the power lines on your right. Moorland track leads to a gate – through this and the stream crossing. At a vague track junction after 100m keep **L** and plunge downhill to another gate. Through this and **SA** to drop down to the road (A57) by the Ladybower Inn (recommended). Turn **R** onto the A57 and **L** at the traffic lights to return to Heatherdene.

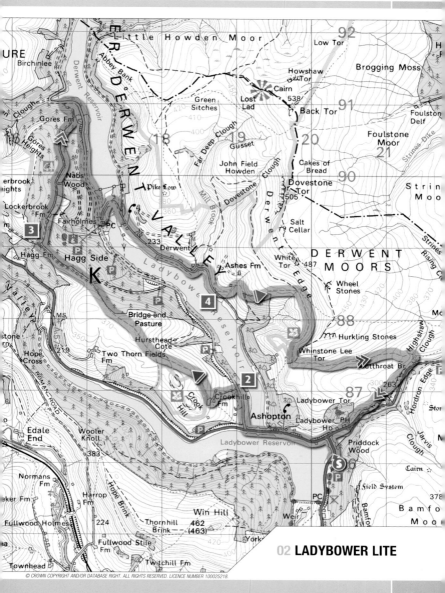

02 **LADYBOWER LITE**

KIM AND TIM RUSSON BEGIN THE CLIMB UP MAGDALEN ROAD

Introduction

Short, fast, fun and almost entirely lacking in level ground. A good introduction to mountain biking, or as a quick training circuit – excellent whatever the weather or season and highly recommended as a night ride. This circuit is away from the main honeypots of the Peak and so has a little more mystery than usually encountered. Plus any route with moorland singletrack is worth getting out of bed for.

The Ride

The route gets better and better the further around you get, which is good news as from the start you're straight into a long tarmac hill climb. Things improve quickly as the route drops down Harden Hill into... the middle of nowhere. Back on the tarmac for a brief climb, the going gets increasingly rough, joining a wild moorland singletrack section before crossing the Holmfirth to Mossley Road (A635) once more. The fantastic long, descending track back to the car park is a fitting finale.

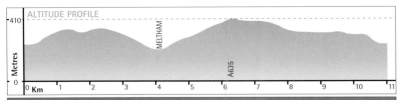

DIGLEY CIRCUIT   **GRADE:** ▲

TOTAL DISTANCE: 11.5KM » **TOTAL ASCENT**: 380M » **TIME**: 1–2 HOURS » **START/FINISH**: DIGLEY RESERVOIR CAR PARK
START GRID REF: SE 109068 » **SATNAV**: HOLMBRIDGE » **PUB**: FORD INN, ON THE A635, TEL: 01484 854 741
CAFÉ: BRING SANDWICHES!

Directions – Digley Circuit

➊ Turn **L** out of Digley Reservoir car park and ride across the dam to a T-junction. Turn **L** onto a road climb for 1.3km, keeping **SA** on Green Gate Road. Turn **L** at the junction with the main road (A635). Follow the main road for 400m to a signed bridleway on the **R**. Follow this right of way, past mounds of earth to join a long, rutted and loose descent to Royd Bridge.

2 Turn **L** along the road and climb on this. Ignore a bridleway that leads straight ahead and instead turn **R** onto another bridleway, passing farms on the left and right. Continue **SA** as road turns to track and pass through a gate by a farm onto wild, moorland singletrack ascending Round Hill. Called Magdalen Road, this singletrack, although often faint (keep the wall to your left to aid navigation) is rideable in dry conditions, if a little technical in places. Eventually the gate at the summit is reached and a short descent past another gate leads to the A635.

3 Turn **R** then almost immediately **L** down the track of Springs Road (signposted *Public Bridleway*) and follow this paved track to a sharp **L** turn just before a gate and stile. Continue around to the **L** and down this superb fast descent along Nether Lane for 2.5km. The track eventually climbs gently to a gate and then a road – turn **R** onto this. At a crossroads turn **R** downhill and cross the dam to return to the car park.

◀━☺⊃ Making a day of it

This ride can be extended either before or after the main loop by heading south from Digley Reservoir and picking up the wide trail that loops through Holme Woods just off the A6024. A tough byway climb after Riding Wood Reservoir leads eventually to Arrunden and a steep tarmac descent down to Holmbridge. Climb on tarmac again to the reservoir.

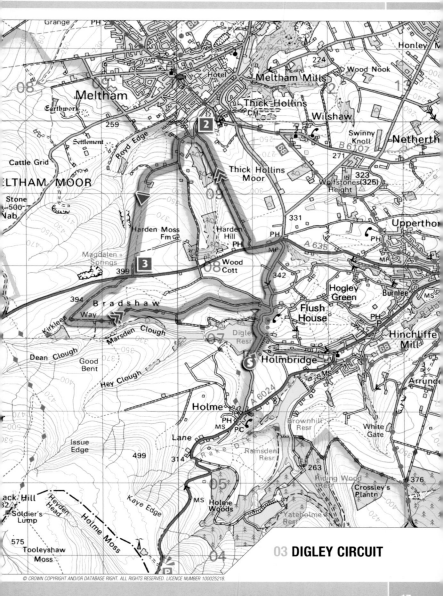

03 **DIGLEY CIRCUIT**

THE CLIMB FROM NORTH AMERICA PHOTO: TIM RUSSON

Introduction

The car park, visitor centre and manicured woodland trails around Langsett Reservoir make up just a few minutes of this figure-of-8 circuit. Gearing up in the pine-wooded car park it might feel like you're at a forest trail centre but, be warned: this route pushes the rider into two tough, remote stretches of moorland trails, and, at times, especially when the weather is blowing in, it can feel like very wild mountain biking indeed. All in all the experiences to be gained riding around Langsett are very real and very rewarding. The ride is included here amongst the more modest classics, as it can easily be shortened into two smaller, but no less poor circuits, both featuring a big moorland experience.

The Ride

From Langsett Visitor Centre car park, skirt south around the pretty Langsett Reservoir and pick up the fine moorland trail from North America Farm to the legendary Cut Gate trail. Top speed down this – whooping and hollering all the way – to a rocky tumble and a stream crossing. Pick up a wild, ancient bridleway across to the Woodhead Pass road, and up the challenging, rutted climb of The Snow Road. The reward for all that hard work is a terrific singletrack descent to Upper Windleden Reservoir, where after a climb up to and descent down to the Trans Pennine Trail leads to a welcome blast along this disused railway. Another pleasant moorland crossing follows and a cathartic spin along hardpack trails back to the car park. An optional short cut is included that gives a fine 9km ride around Langsett and Cut Gate, which, thanks to Yorkshire Water, now features only a few hundred metres of tarmac.

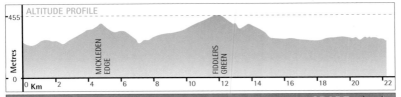

ALTITUDE PROFILE

455

Metres

0

0 Km 2 4 6 8 10 12 14 16 18 20 22

MICKLEDEN EDGE

FIDDLERS GREEN

LANGSETT   **GRADE:** ▲ » ▲

TOTAL DISTANCE: 9KM/22KM » **TOTAL ASCENT**: 600M » **TIME**: 3–4 HOURS » **START/FINISH**: LANGSETT VISITOR CENTRE
START GRID REF: SE 210004 » **SATNAV**: S36 4GY » **PUB**: THE WAGGON & HORSES, LANGSETT, TEL: 01226 763 147
CAFÉ: BANK VIEW CAFÉ, LANGSETT, TEL: 01226 762 337

MICKLEDEN EDGE PHOTO: TIM RUSSON

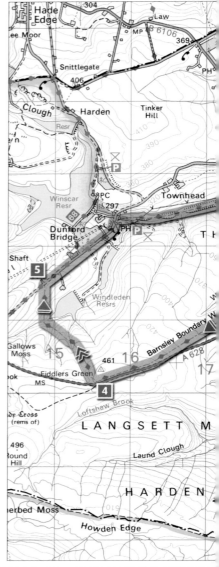

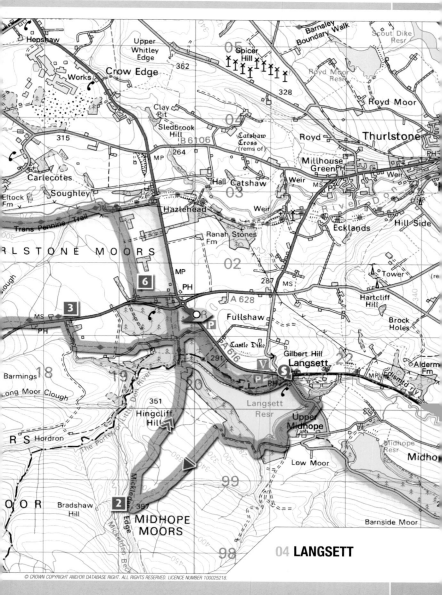

04 LANGSETT

Directions – Langsett

➊ Locate a track along the western (right, facing in) edge of the car park. At a track junction at the corner of the field, descend on a cycleway towards the reservoir and bear **L** at the bottom, with the reservoir now on your right. At the road, pass through a gate and turn **R** onto Midhope Cliff Lane and follow this across the reservoir dam. Approx. 150m after the reservoir look out for a track on your **R** – signed *Public Bridleway* – and take this. As the woodland ends on the right look out for a small gate signed *Yorkshire Water Permissive Path* (also entrance to permissive bridleway). Turn **R** through this and fork **L** after 20m onto signed *Permissive Bridleway*. Follow this across clearing and down into woods. Descend and traverse the hillside before emerging at a wide track just below a gate – Thickwoods Lane (unsigned). Turn **R** and follow the track through woodland, through two gates and then up and along the side of the woods to the ruins of North America Farm. Turn **L before the gate** to join a fine moorland ascent (wall on right). Continue **SA** across moor for 1.5km to a T-junction with the Cut Gate path.

➋ Turn **R** down Mickleden Edge (Cut Gate) and follow loose, stony path, mainly in descent. Descent continues, dropping into steeper, rocky section before track smoothes out and drops to a footbridge – get into low gear before gate. Go through gate, cross bridge and tackle short, sharp climb up stony track opposite. At the top of the climb follow the main track **SA** to a track junction on the left after approx. 300m.* Turn **L** here (signed *Public Bridleway – Swinden*). Pass through two gates and fork **R** at track T-junction onto walled lane. After approx. 150m look out for a bridleway on the **R** signed to *Bordhill* – take this. Ride **SA** through gates on a walled track. At final gate, after which double track weaves left, turn **R** and ride up to the busy main road (A628).

*Short Cut: 9km Loop
Alternatively, continue **SA** and, after 200m, turn **R** on signed track back to car park.

➌ Turn **L** and ride the left-hand verge up to the Dog and Partridge Inn (it being a grouse moor hereabouts). **Cross the road with care** – I'd recommend pushing across – and through the gate to pick up the grassy, rutted track (The Snow Road) out onto the moor. The gradient eases but the ruts can be a nightmare to track – singletrack hell. The trail eventually swings back to the road – keep **SA** following the now broken singletrack, boggy in places, over the summit of South Nab. Look out for a *Bridleway* sign pointing **R**.

4 Turn **R**, heading away from the road and onto a stretch of fine, bleak, moorland singletrack. Fork **L** at a split in the trail just before a wall and open gateway, as the descent starts to the reservoir. Drop down to the reservoir headwaters and follow the boggy climb back up to the road.

5 Turn **R** and descend the road looking out for a **R** turn onto the Trans Pennine Trail in the valley bottom. Turn **R** onto this and spin along the disused railway for approx. 3km. Pass under the electricity wires and **STOP** just before going under a concrete bridge. The next 50m or so are footpath **so please carry/push your bike**: Take the discrete steps on the **L** just before the bridge, cross the bridge, turn **L**, and then go **R** through the gate onto the moor. Back on the bike, this great bit of trail soon reaches tarmac.

6 Turn **L**, and then take the signed bridleway on the **R**, just before reaching the road. Cross the main road (A628) and ride back into the Langsett trail network. Keep **SA**, rejoining the outward loop, and bear **L** at the track junction. After 200m turn **R** onto signed track back to the car park.

TRACK JUNCTION WITH MICKLEDEN EDGE PHOTO: TIM RUSSON

BRIDLEWAY
Bikes

FOOTPATH
Walkers

Introduction

A very good, relatively short mountain bike route that makes the most of the sensational riding along the ridge that connects Mam Tor and Rushup Edge. Two of the four significant climbs are made on tarmac, the other two are off-road and only really steep in short, rideable sections. Play your cards right and in good, dry conditions this whole route should be manageable without a foot down by the fit and able rider, but it would still be a challenge. Maintenance work on the trails around Mam Tor by the national park and volunteers add to the enduring splendour of this ride.

The Ride

Out of Castleton we head up via the wrinkled, collapsing tarmac below Odin's Mine. After some easy road work, we pass through the gate and climb up onto Rushup Edge to enjoy some spectacular scenery. Crossing remote ground near the end of the ridge brings us to Chapel Gate – a fast descent of great character – do you dare commit to the exposed ridges of decaying tarmac or do you rattle down the stony ruts? Another road climb brings us stalwartly to Mam Nick; don't worry we lose that height again very, very quickly on the rutted run down to Greenlands. Then of course it's straight back up to Hollins Cross on a cleanable climb before dropping over the other side on the fast and tricky descent back to Castleton. It's over much too soon, but your legs and arms will know they've been for a ride.

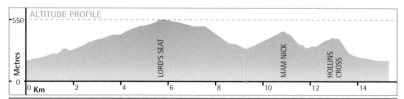

MAM TOR FIGURE-OF-8   **GRADE:** ▲

TOTAL DISTANCE: 15.5KM » **TOTAL ASCENT**: 660M » **TIME**: 1.5-2.5 HOURS » **START/FINISH**: CASTLETON CAR PARK
START GRID REF: SK 149830 » **SATNAV**: S33 8WN » **PUB**: PLENTY TO CHOOSE FROM IN CASTLETON
CAFÉ: THREE ROOFS CAFÉ, TEL: 01433 620 533

Directions – Mam Tor Figure-of-8

➊ Turn **R** out of the main Castleton car park at the mini roundabout and follow the A6187 up the valley towards Mam Tor, ignoring the left fork uphill to Winnats Pass. Continue **SA** past Treak Cliff Cavern and **SA** again past the bus turning area. Climb up on steep tarmac through a gate and continue up the collapsing tarmac road to a gate at the top – watch out for drop offs! Continue along a short stretch of road to join the main road and turn **R**. Follow the road for 500m and turn **R** steeply uphill just past a parking area. Follow the road, looking out for a gate on the **L** just before Mam Nick.

2 Pass through the gate (signposted *Rushup Edge*) and begin a tough climb. Continue climbing, passing through a gate and up onto Rushup Edge. Continue **SA** along a vague level track through several gateways – always keeping the wall to your right – until the path swerves **R** through a gate.

3 Go through the gate and descend **L** to a fork in the path. Fork **R** (signposted *To Edale Via Barber Booth*) along a superb, exposed track across moorland, soon descending with great interest via a broken track with decaying tarmac ridges – this is Chapel Gate. Keep on this track through a gate to meet the road at the bottom. Turn **R** up the road and climb for 1.5km. Look out for a wooden gate on the **L** by a bus stop and lay-by (almost at the col).

4 Pass through the gate and bear **L** almost immediately down a stony shoot to another gate. Through this onto a steep, rutted descent, eventually leading to another gate. Go through this and descend quickly to a gate by a road and dwelling (Greenlands). **Do not pass through gate**, instead continue **SA**, initially on pleasant gravel singletrack. Commence climbing, which continues with increasing difficulty up through two gates, then into particularly challenging section up to the ridge top crossroads at Hollins Cross.

5 Bear **L** on the ridge at Hollins Cross and ride uphill briefly looking out for a blue bridleway arrow pointing off to the right-hand side of the main track. Follow this fork to a narrow gate, through this to a second gate and downhill across the hillside. Shortly after a collapsed wall the path forks – bear **R** downhill and follow the path onto a sunken path to meet a gate at the bottom (footpath joins from right). Go through the gate and down a rocky singletrack – one last test! Join Hollowford Road and follow tarmac **SA** (ignore right turn to Conference Centre) to join the A6187 in Castleton. Turn **R** to return to the car park.

**05 MAM TOR
FIGURE-OF-8**

SECTION 2

Epics

Getting longer, Epics require that bit more time and effort. The difficulty varies, but all feature a mix of fast, technical and tough riding that covers some interesting ground and is not to be underestimated. Allow a few hours and enjoy some of the best riding the Peak has to offer.

Epics
sponsored by

www.sealskinz.com

THE CLIMB FROM HOLLINS CROSS TO MAM TOR (ROUTE 13)

CATHERINE BOWMAN ON BRADWELL EDGE SINGLETRACK PHOTO: TIM RUSSON

06 Bradwell Circuit – Hope Valley

21km

Introduction

A great ride on the southern side of the Hope Valley. Although just fitting onto the Dark Peak map, this route is mainly on limestone, so prepare yourself for a little less grip on the rocks beneath your tyres. The drainage en route is generally good, so expect it to be in condition all year round.

Incorporating quite a bit of steady mileage, this route does throw in a couple of tough and techy downhills – and there's an option to explore the Pin Dale 'Drop Zone' too...

The Ride

Starting from Hope, the route warms up nicely along the main road before a gruelling tarmac/gravel ascent up onto Shatton Moor. It then takes a big, wide circle around the head of Over Dale. The first real descent is a little awkward to spot, but it's well worth finding and it drops you, exhilarated, into Bradwell. The next section behind Hope Valley Cement Works is unusual to say the least – a bit like mountain biking through the location of a cheap 70s sci-fi TV series. Then it's steeply up on back roads and around some impressive holes in the ground to meet up with the Limestone Way and, eventually, a very demanding descent through Cave Dale. All that remains now is a little more road work back up to, and down, Pin Dale before returning to Hope and a brew in the Woodbine.

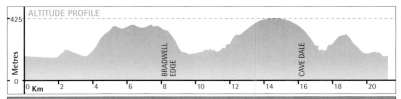

TOTAL DISTANCE: 21KM » TOTAL ASCENT: 800M » TIME: 2–3 HOURS » START/FINISH: HOPE VILLAGE CAR PARK
START GRID REF: SK 171834 » SATNAV: S33 6RD » PUB: TRAVELLERS REST, BROUGH, TEL: 01433 620 363
CAFÉ: WOODBINE CAFÉ, HOPE, TEL: 07778 113 882

CAVE DALE

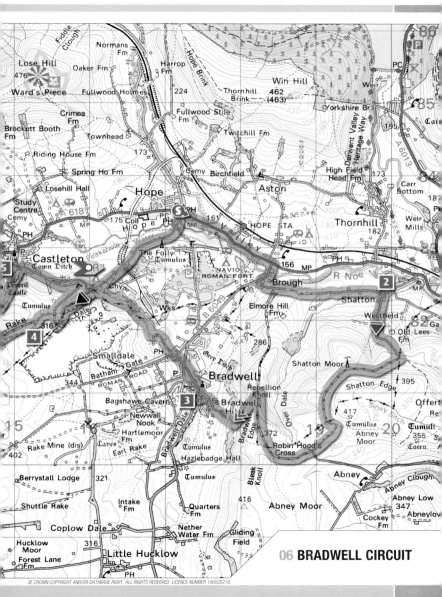

06 **BRADWELL CIRCUIT**

Directions – Bradwell Circuit

→ Turn **R** out of Hope car park and ride along the A6187 towards Hathersage for just under 2km. Turn **R** at the traffic lights next to the pub onto the B6049 and follow this for 200m before turning **L** onto Brough Lane, just before a narrow road bridge. Climb up the steep hill on tarmac, and keep **SA** onto track where the road bends off right. Continue **SA** through gates to join a tarmac road and follow it **L** to descend into Shatton.

2 Cross the ford and turn **R** up a long steep climb on tarmac. Keep uphill onto the track, past the mast and track levels off to a gate. Bear **L** over more eroded tracks, soon curving back **R** around Over Dale. A good track starts to descend **BUT** look out for a gate on the **L** (with old rusty latch and *Bridleway* sign) after 500m (easy to miss). Turn **L** through the gate, and ride diagonally across the field on a small track to a gate. Go through the gate, keep **R** along the wall and bear **L** for a good, exciting descent into Bradwell (muddy in winter). Keep **R** and turn **R** onto the B6049.

3 Descend through the village, go through the lights and after 500m fork **L** onto Town Lane, just before the football field. Ride **SA** at the crossroads up a track to a gate. Turn **R** down a path onto a bridleway leading down into the quarry. Keep **SA** at all junctions, following waymarks leading across quarry roads. Stay with this bridleway to its end at a road. Turn **L**, climb steeply up a track past Pin Dale Quarry (motocross playground all around you here – some good drop-offs, jumps etc. to be had, but handle with care!). Turn **R** at the top and then turn **L** onto the road. Follow the road up past a left-hand bend and turn **R** onto the wide Dirtlow Rake track just before a cattle grid.

4 Follow the track parallel to the road and then up and away from road. Ride **SA** along a track past a large quarry to your right and **SA** through a gate. At a bridleway crossroads, take the track through a gate on the **R**. Follow this track across a field signposted *Castleton*, bearing down and slightly **R** towards a small gate in a drystone wall (ignore 4WD tracks leading off up and ahead). Go through the gate and follow the track down and **L** into Cave Dale, keeping the wall on your left to a gate. Go through the gate – track becomes very steep and very rocky (full-on trials skills required for success!), eventually easing as dale opens out. Continue **SA** to gate.

5 Go through another gate and turn **R** up the road to an acute fork. Fork **R*** and follow the road steeply uphill to a **L** turn for the descent of Pin Dale (revenge for the earlier climb!). From the base of Pin Dale continue **SA** crossing the railway cutting and bear **L** over the stream into Hope. Bear **L** to the car park.

*Short cut – Misses out Pin Dale descent

OR *Fork **L** and ride slightly up and then down to a junction. Bear **L**, then continue **SA** crossing railway cutting. Bear **L** over the stream into Hope. Bear **L** to the car park.

BRADWELL EDGE PHOTO: TIM RUSSON

07 Disley Circuit – West Peak

23km

Introduction

This great big loop around New Mills uses a cunningly-linked network of trails – consisting of rocky byways, ancient farm tracks and fast hardpack trails – to take in a variety of superb terrain. With the emphasis on climbing, this demanding route is a very good test of fitness. This ride features all manner of remnants from the industrial revolution – mines, mills and quarries – of course you'll not notice these, as you'll need to keep your eye on your line. Not without reason is it one of my favourite rides.

The Ride

From Disley Station (various parking available) this route climbs out above the town, soon dropping down into the congested Goyt Valley, before climbing back up towards Chinley Churn where commanding views of the entire route can be enjoyed. We then drop into, and climb out of, the Sett Valley before the route swings north, contouring around New Mills. An excellent descent follows back into the Goyt Valley and then a final climb returns you to Disley.

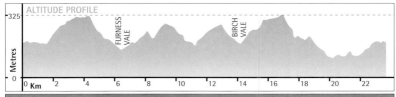

DISLEY CIRCUIT   GRADE: ▲ » ▲

TOTAL DISTANCE: 23KM » **TOTAL ASCENT**: 820M » **TIME**: 2–3 HOURS » **START/FINISH**: DISLEY STATION
START GRID REF: SK 972845 » **SATNAV**: SK12 2AE » **PUB**: THE FOX INN, BROOK BOTTOM, TEL: 0161 427 1634
CAFÉ: BRING SANDWICHES!

SINGLETRACK UP FROM GOWHOLE

07 DISLEY CIRCUIT

Directions – Disley Circuit

➤ Leaving Disley Station car park, head east out of the town centre on the busy A6 for approx 1.25km. Turn **R** up Greenshall Lane (track just past & opposite remains of Little Chef – RIP, currently the Purple Pakora restaurant, but this is likely to change!), hard climbing follows, initially on very loose, rocky surface then farm track for 1km to the road at the top. Turn **L** onto the road for 2km, passing Easter Cottage on the right, to an unsigned doubletrack bridleway through a gate on the **L**. Descend bridleway to Furness Vale, passing Diglee Farm. Continue **SA** along farm track to join tarmac. Turn **L** at the bottom to meet the A6. Cross this **(take care)**, continue **SA** past Furness Vale railway station and continue descent on tarmac to take sharp **R** turn on tarmac as road starts to ascend after Goyt Bridge.

2 After 500m take the signposted bridleway **L** (a little way past railway bridge, on bend in road). Take the **L** fork (right is to the farm) and follow doubletrack then rocky path on **R**, just past Howcroft Farm – a steady climb – to meet the road. Turn **L** and descend steeply on tarmac to a signposted bridleway on the **R**. Turn **R** here and ride **SA** past cottage on left. **SA** through a gate and climb easily up grassy track through fields, stream on your left. Go through a gate through Hollinhurst Head Farm and continue **SA** up to meet main track at Moor Lodge.

3 Turn **L** on fast descent past quarry on right to Birch Vale. Turn **R** on main road and then sharp **L** opposite The Grouse (in the direction of Thornsett). Cross River Sett, then take bridleway on **R** – stiff climb on a variety of surfaces takes you up to road.

4 Turn **L** and climb steeply for 400m to brow of hill. Turn **R** past quarry onto farm track. Pass farm with lots of barking dogs and take first bridleway on **L** (signposted *No Motor Vehicles Except for Access by Agricultural Vehicles*) – initially a grassy doubletrack through gate, then a very pleasant descent down walled path joining tarmac to pass Aspenshaw Hall. Continue **SA** downhill at road junction then make steep tarmac climb past Lydiate Farm and Blake Hall on right for 1km. Turn **L** up rocky bridleway (opposite Briargrove Farm), follow this, mainly uphill, to road.

5 Turn **R** on tarmac and then **L** after 100m up a rocky track along the edge of woodland to a four-way junction. Continue **SA** along track. After 750m turn **L** onto track (Black Lane) and follow this to its end (currently very loose) at a three-way junction with farm tracks, just below a large cross up and left. Ride **SA** at junction – metalled road soon becomes bumpy – and continue past a couple of posh dwellings on left and ignore left turn. Bumpy track continues downhill and curves **L** (next to golf course on right). Follow very loose path steeply downwards just **R** of where track turns left into dwelling, then almost immediately turn **L** through gateway – track stays very loose as it drops down and out at T-junction past more posh dwellings. Got that? Phew!

6 Turn **L** to join fairly rocky track and fast descent. Ignore acute right turn where rocky track meets better surface. Climb up **SA**, then make short descent into Brook Bottom. Turn **R** then **L** past The Fox Inn (yes, it is an excellent pub).

7 Turn **R**, just after the pub, to follow a wide track (signposted *Goyt Way*) – excellent fast descent past Strines Station (alternative start). Continue **SA** down the road past a lake on the right and over a bridge to reach junction with B6101. Turn **L** along the road for 1km to a bridleway on the **R** (this is a small path just past a private road, opposite Lych Cottage, just before bridge). A muddy path leads along the river, past the paper mill to reach a road out of the mill. Bear **R** up tarmac road and turn **R** under railway track, continue climbing over canal and under the second railway bridge to the A6. Turn **R** along the A6 back to Disley Station.

08 The Beast

20km

Introduction

The world is divided into those who love descending The Beast and those who don't have six inches of travel and a full-face helmet. Making up less than ten minutes of this circumnavigation of Win Hill, the rocky, bouldery bridleway descending north from the col between Kinder Scout and Win Hill is a serious challenge. Loose rocks, large rocks and drop-offs are the norm, while a successful line through the two main bends is difficult on first acquaintance. The rest of the route is pleasant in comparison, a fast hardpack ride along the shores of Ladybower, an excursion through the pines of Woodlands Valley, a great climb up onto Hope Brink and of course the rocky climb out of Hope and a return via the same superb scramble. The Beast rewards the confident, and punishes the over confident. The wary can rest assured; even the author has been known to take it steady on the rough bits.

The Ride

From the mountain bike capital of the Dark Peak – Hope – head out along Edale, to climb up the surprisingly-rideable rocky track onto the shoulder of Win Hill. Passing Hope Cross, descend *the* track – known locally as The Beast – to the shores of Ladybower, continue around the reservoir, and along a short section of disused railway before climbing up once again onto Win Hill, for the sole purpose of the spectacular rocky descent back to Hope.

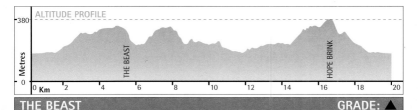

THE BEAST   GRADE: ▲

TOTAL DISTANCE: 20KM » **TOTAL ASCENT:** 720M » **TIME:** 2 HOURS » **START/FINISH:** PAY AND DISPLAY CAR PARK, HOPE VILLAGE » **START GRID REF:** SK 171834 » **SATNAV:** S33 6RD » **PUB:** THE CHESHIRE CHEESE, EDALE ROAD, HOPE, **TEL:** 01433 620 381 » **CAFÉ:** WOODBINE CAFÉ & B&B, HOPE, TEL: 07778 113 882

Directions – The Beast

⑤ Turn **R** out of the car park and take the first **L** signed *Edale*. After nearly 2km, bear **R** – effectively **SA** – up Fullwood Stile Lane, just after crossing the bridge on the bend. Follow the lane, eventually through a gate and onto a rocky track.

2 Keep **SA** through a gate, past Hope Cross and through the next gate. Turn **R** at the bridleway crossroads – this is the start of The Beast. A fast and initially-steady descent leads alongside woods to another gate: at this point you may want to lower your seat and say a short prayer before heading into the woods. The start is tough, and the bends require courage and a good choice of line. All too soon it's over, one way or another. The Beast spits you out at the head of Ladybower Reservoir; follow the track around the shore, looking out for a bridleway (signed) heading **R** up into the woods. Take this, steep at first, before it levels off and finally descends once again to the shoreline.

3 Follow the track and keep **SA** down the road, ignoring the left turn across the dam. After 100m take the bridleway on the **R** – The Thornhill Trail – and follow this to the road. Turn **R** along the road into Thornhill. Turn **R** in the village by the phone box, following Carr Lane (signed *Unsuitable for Motor Vehicles*) to the village of Aston. Keep **SA** and at the brow of the second dip in the road turn **R** uphill signposted *Win Hill*.

4 Follow the lane, turning **L** at Edge Farm along the sunken lane, through two gates to emerge into a field. Cross this to a small gate and keep on the bridleway as it contours around, then up through another gate following a delightful rising trail onto the broad ridge of Win Hill. Keep **SA** to descend, on a multitude of singletracks, ruts and paths to eventually hit a gate. **Don't go through it**, but hairpin **L** and retrace your outward route back to Hope.

◄⊂⊙⊃ Making a day of it
When it comes to links, the world is almost your oyster with this route. You could link north into either of the **Ladybower** rides (pages 11 and 63), or link south into the **Bradwell Circuit** (page 33) or the **Hathersage Circuit** (page 91).

◄⊂⊙⊃ Making a weekend of it
Stay in the Woodbine for the weekend and go nuts on the amazing riding around the Hope Valley. Loads of routes to choose from, including this one, **Mam Tor Figure-of-8** (page 25), **Hope Valley Watershed** (page 79) and **Hope Tour** (page 121), among others.

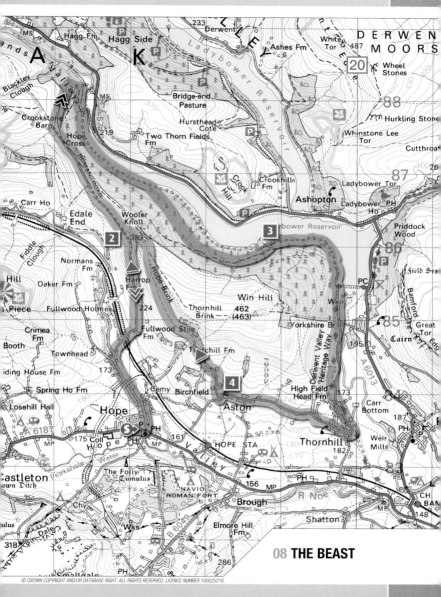

08 **THE BEAST**

THE DROP FROM OLLERSETT TO HAYFIELD

09 Chinley Churn & Rowarth — West Peak 21.7km

Introduction

Taking in two quiet outposts of the Peak District National Park, this loop ignores the hoards of mountain bikers on the High Peak pilgrimage and instead offers quality singletrack, rocky bridleways and fast hardpack on the western fringe of the National Park. The ride can conveniently be split into two short blasts – a Chinley Circuit and a Rowarth Circuit, ideal for an evening – but ridden in its entirety it gives great riding, rewarding views and a taste of life in the backwaters of the High Peak. Chinley Churn, for reasons I'm yet to fully understand, is one of my favourite places in the Peak District; maybe it's the solitude, maybe the views down on the industrial past, or perhaps it's those swooping descents.

The Ride

Our circuit takes in the best of Chinley Churn, and the bridleways around the village of Rowarth, which is allegedly only accessible on a mountain bike! Starting from the Sett Valley we ride the western slopes of Lantern Pike, to an amazing rocky tumble down to Rowarth. Another good descent after a little road work leads to more deserted lanes, merging into pleasant, fast farm tracks and a stiff climb over the eastern slopes of Lantern Pike. A great descent leads back down into the Sett Valley, and then a steady climb up to Chinley Churn. This track is followed right around The Churn, to pick up the trail climbing back up over the summit. This wilderness trail swoops down, and then picks out a classic descent into Foxholes Clough. A track, and one of those annoying grassy fields, leads to more rocky fun on a brilliant, seldom-used trail into the back streets of Hayfield.

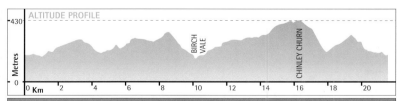

ALTITUDE PROFILE

430

Metres

BIRCH VALE

CHINLEY CHURN

0 Km   2   4   6   8   10   12   14   16   18   20

CHINLEY CHURN & ROWARTH   GRADE: ▲

TOTAL DISTANCE: 21.7KM » **TOTAL ASCENT**: 780M » **TIME**: 2–3 HOURS » **START/FINISH**: HAYFIELD SETT VALLEY TRAIL CAR PARK » **START GRID REF**: SK 036869 » **SATNAV**: SK22 2ES » **PUB**: KINDER LODGE, HAYFIELD, TEL: 01663 743 613 **CAFÉ**: MOST OF THE LOCAL PUBS SERVE UP A GOOD SANDWICH

Directions — Chinley Churn & Rowarth

➜ Head east out of the car park, towards Hayfield, cross the busy road and turn **L** on the main road through the centre of Hayfield. Follow this lane, taking the **L** fork in the lane, under the road and ride past the houses, then steeply uphill. Keep following the lane and, as it levels off, take the lane on the **R** just after the mast. Follow the farm track, past the barking dogs, and keep **L** at the junction on a great rocky descent to a lane. Follow this past the impressive Mill Inn. Continue on the tarmac, turn **L** after the Inn and take the first **R**, back into Rowarth Village. (There is a bridleway that cuts this corner off but it is not recommended in this direction.)

2 Link up with a bridleway on another fine descent to a ford, cross this and follow the lane **SA** looking out for a track on the **R** signed *Pennine Bridleway*. Follow this uphill and stay with it as it turns **R**, keeping **SA** at the junction of tracks by Matley Moor Farm, to enter and cross the field heading for the gate and track on the opposite side. Go through the gate and up the steep lane, climbing over Lantern Pike. A steep descent leads back down to a lane.

3 Go more or less **SA** (**R** and immediately **L**) onto a small bridleway. A good little descent leads down to the road. Turn **L** at the road and follow this up to the main road and turn **R**. After 300m bear **L** up a steep tarmac lane — Over Hill Road — past the quarries. Continue climbing and keep **SA** as the road turns to track. As the track emerges at the apex of a hairpin bend, bear **L** — effectively **SA** — and follow the road uphill for approx. 200m. Turn sharp **L** onto a bridleway track by a house.

4 Follow this for almost 2km, steeply at first, then rutty and fun over Chinley Churn. Ignore the first bridleway off to the right at a gate but continue **SA** — effectively **L** after the gate — on a swoopy and rutted descent. Look out for a vague bridleway on the **R** that crests the shoulder of the hillside (photo previous page) — take this. (If you reach a point where the track meets a wall on the right, then you've missed it!) Drop down this fast trail and turn **R** downhill at the T-junction. Keep **SA** into the trees and **SA** — all very downhill — to the farm. Follow the track down to the stream and climb back up to the road. **SA** across the road and follow the track to a gate. Turn **R** up the road for approx. 200m, looking out for a bridleway on the **L**, opposite a house. Take this lane, and follow it to a gate and ride **SA** into the field. Follow the posts, heading for the right-hand edge of the trees. At the trees, go through the gate and downhill — quite technical with a few tricky bits. Turn **L** at the bridleway T-junction. More superb singletrack in descent leads to the valley bottom. Follow this into Hayfield and so back to the start.

09 CHINLEY CHURN & ROWARTH

DROPPING FROM COWN EDGE

10 Misty Marple

22.3km

Introduction

The perfect ride! Nowhere are the hills so long or so technical that the average rider shouldn't be able to ride them, the descents are fun but not hair-raising and the terrain is beautifully varied. Altogether this is actually one of the more amenable rides in the Dark Peak. Halfway round on the ride the fine viewpoint of Cown Edge is reached. From here the ride is basically downhill all the way, what better way to enjoy the view.

I chose to start from sleepy hollow that is Strines Station, the disadvantage being that you hit the two main hills without any warm-up. Perhaps a better start is from parking at the Roman Lakes, just north, then the buzz along the Goyt Way provides a great warm-up. But I just like Strines; it's quiet and somehow deserves to be the starting point of a great adventure.

The Ride

From Strines the ride climbs out of the deep Goyt Valley, and up again onto the ancient high pastures above New Mills. From here one can see over the valley to Lantern Pike, and yes, the ride does drop down and climb back up to the flank of the hill. A fine descent into Rowarth follows, with a bit of tarmac leading to another fine descent. Tarmac and ancient trackways lead to the summit of Cown Edge, after which it's fun-fun-fun pedalling tracks, singletrack, rocky descents and hardpack, with a touch of the black top back to the start.

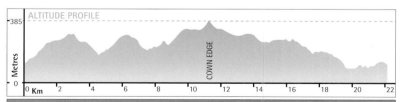

MISTY MARPLE   GRADE: ▲

TOTAL DISTANCE: 22.3KM » **TOTAL ASCENT**: 710M » **TIME**: 2.5-3 HOURS » **START/FINISH**: STRINES STATION
START GRID REF: SJ 978864 » **SATNAV**: STRINES (NEAREST) » **PARKING**: ON THE COBBLES STATION APPROACH
PUB: THE FOX INN, BROOK BOTTOM, TEL: 0161 427 1634 » **CAFÉ**: TWO STRUDEL-FLAVOURED MULE BARS SHOULD DO IT

CLIMBING UP COWN EDGE

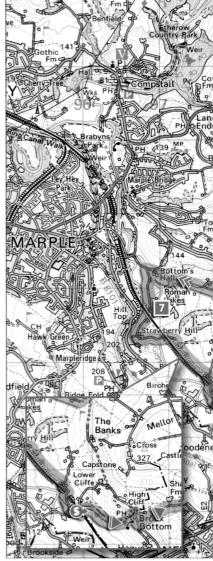

10 MISTY MARPLE

Directions – Misty Marple

1 Head up the cobbled lane and take the track **L** of the station entrance. Follow this uphill through beautiful woodland, soon steepening with a challenging finale before reaching The Fox Inn at Brook Bottom. Turn **R** uphill on tarmac and then **L** after 100m up a rocky bridleway – persistence pays off as it soon eases. You now have the hardest climbs behind you. Follow this lane to a road and turn **L**.

2 Climb on tarmac for 1km to a track crossroads. Turn **R** onto an excellent rocky descent, with woodland to your left. Turn **R** at the road and then sharp **L** after 100m onto a signposted bridleway above a farm. Descend to a road and turn **R**. Follow this, losing the last bit of all your height gained earlier, and keep **SA** where the road turns right. Follow the lane **SA** *(No turning space)* past Aspenshaw Hall. The lane gives way to pleasant singletrack ascent and, as woodland turns to moorland, middle ring gives way to granny ring.

3 Go through a gate and turn **L** onto a track. Follow this, keeping **L** at the junction on a great rocky descent to a lane and follow this past the impressive Mill Inn. Continue on the tarmac, turn **L** after the Inn and take the first **R**, back into Rowarth Village. (There is a bridleway that cuts this corner off but is not recommended in this direction.) Keep **SA**, the lane narrows and gets a bit steep, eventually cresting the hill before turning into a fast track, descending to a fine water splash and gate.

4 **SA** up the lane for 1.5km. When the tarmac turns sharp right, head **L** on the farm track. Follow this until it splits, go through the gate and up the steep decaying **R** fork to the crest of Cown Edge. Savour the view towards Manchester while ragging it downhill through the odd gate, past Robin Hood's Picking Rods (no, I've no idea either) to the road. Turn **L**.

5 Follow the road for 2.5km, past a pub, past roads to the left and right, and then take the farm track on the **R** (it's the only one to look out for). Follow this, under the electricity wires, and up to a T-junction. Turn **R** and follow the lane **SA** to reach a gate. Go through this and across the field, back onto a track to arrive at a graveyard – quite spooky if night riding. Turn **L** down the lane to the main road in Mellor. Turn **L** on the main road and immediately **R** up Gibb Lane.

6 Follow the lane to the hamlet of Tarden. Keep **SA** to the golf course and **SA** past the clubhouse towards the Scout camp. Just after the Scout camp, look out for a rocky track descending to the **R**, vaguely signed *Marple*. Descend this, then follow the lane with the lake on your right, looking out for a sharp **L**, signed *Lakes Rd*, to the main lake. Take this and follow it, lakes now on your left.

7 Follow this lane – the Goyt Way – as it weaves along the valley, past mysterious homesteads, relics of the industrial revolution and interestingly-named buildings. The odd, intriguing bridleway occasionally joins from the left, but keeping on the main track one will eventually appear at the bottom of the cobbled lane leading up to Strines Station.

THE ROCKY CLIMB OUT OF BROOK BOTTOM

11 Snake Doctor – West Peak

16km

Introduction

Short and very, very sharp would be the best way to describe this route. Very useful as an afternoon training route if you're local to the area, this route will test both uphill endurance and, even more, your ability to handle a potentially very dangerous descent!

The road climb up the Snake Pass, is basically quite safe, the visibility is good for cars, so you and your bike can be seen, don't try to draft some of the roadies up here, some of them are seriously smooth. Ironically the descent of Doctor's Gate is at least as tiring as the ascent of the Snake Pass.

The Ride

After a fairly prolonged warm up crossing the notorious Pennine byway of the Snake Pass, this route cuts off into the midst of nowhere via the course of an ancient road. Tough, technical climbing is followed by an even tougher descent that will initially require full-on trials skills for success – approach with caution. The trail is not in the best of condition in places, which will require a few dabs by us mortals. The trail then gradually eases, finishing with a super-fast run on a good track back to civilisation (well, Glossop).

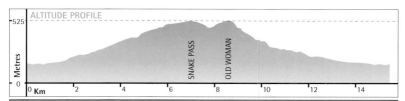

SNAKE DOCTOR

GRADE: △ » ▲

TOTAL DISTANCE: 16KM » **TOTAL ASCENT**: 520M » **TIME**: 2 HOURS » **START/FINISH**: GLOSSOP RAILWAY STATION CAR PARK
START GRID REF: SK 035943 » **SATNAV**: SK13 8BS » **PUB**: RELY ON YOUR WATER BOTTLE » **CAFÉ**: PACK SOME GRUB

Directions – Snake Doctor

➤ Turn **R** out of the car park and **L** at the traffic lights onto Sheffield Road (A57) in the direction of the Snake Pass. Follow this (usually) busy road uphill through good scenery for 8km, passing the Pennine Way footpath after 7km. After a descent of approx. 1km, look out for a bridleway beginning from a layby on the **L** (signposted *Doctor's Gate*).

2 **SA** through gate and follow a track to cross a ford. **SA** along paving flag track to four-way crossroads. **SA** to descend – through gate – on very rough track (Roman Road). Very technical at first, keep the river on your right. Continue **SA** down the track, which eases slightly but continues to throw in some very difficult sections. Approx. 3km from the crossroads, and after crossing the river twice, join a smooth, fast track to a gate. Go through the gate over the **R** bridge (ignore left-hand bridge which leads to farm).

3 After 1.3km and another gate, the track turns near some works into Shepley Street. Follow Shepley Street to T-junction and turn **L** past the post office. At the T-junction turn **R** onto the A57 and retrace your steps back to the station.

⊷☉⊃ Making a day of it
Doctor's Gate features on the day-long Killer, **Bleaklow Circuit** (page 131).

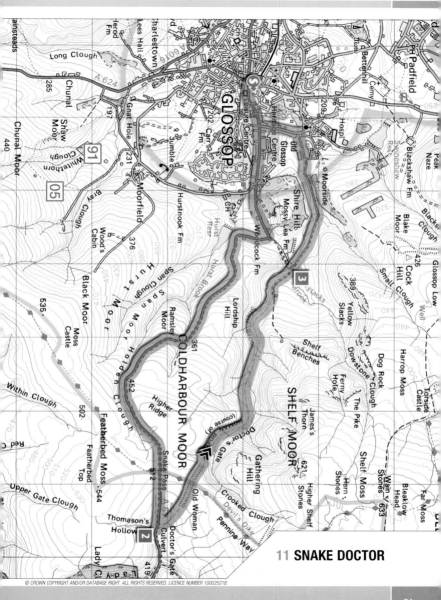

11 SNAKE DOCTOR

12 This is Ladybower

Introduction

Ladybower epitomises the classic Peak District mountain bike circuit. Starting from the idyllic lakeside resort of Fairholmes in the Derwent Valley, this three-up/three-down ride heads off on a high-level round across the shoulders of much of the bulk of the Dark Peak and features a bit of everything; singletrack, rocky descents, woodland trails, remote moorland, views and wildlife. The ride itself feels a lot less demanding than the terrain would dictate – such is the splendour of the landscape – and the pain in the legs is all but forgotten. I never, ever, get tired of this superb ride.

The Ride

The ride starts from Fairholmes – arrive early if you want a parking place at the weekend – alternative parking is available in lay-bys on the road to Fairholmes, or at Heatherdene car park (SK 202859 – a good alternative start). After a quick warm-up spin along the gentle shores of Ladybower Reservoir the route proper kicks in with a great climb up onto the Derwent Moors. This leads to one of the Peak's best descents down to Cutthroat Bridge and the Ladybower Inn. After a brief stint on the road we traverse around the bulk of Win Hill and climb up Hope Brink onto the col between Win Hill and Kinder Scout, a high moorland trail takes one to the very rocky, very brilliant descent into Woodlands Valley. An almost perfect climb back out past Rowlee Farm leads to more great high level trails past Lockerbrook Farm, before the third and final of our great descents down Gores Heights back to the shores of Derwent Reservoir and a freewheel back to the start.

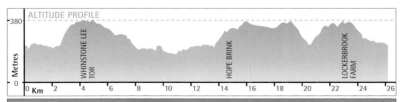

THIS IS LADYBOWER   GRADE: ▲

TOTAL DISTANCE: 26.5KM » **TOTAL ASCENT**: 990M » **TIME**: 2-4 HOURS » **START/FINISH**: FAIRHOLMES (ALTERNATIVE START AT HEATHERDENE) » **START GRID REF**: SK 173893 » **SATNAV**: S33 0AQ (NEAREST)
PUB: LADYBOWER INN, TEL: 01433 651 241 » **CAFÉ**: FAIRHOLMES VISITOR CENTRE, TEL: 01433 650 953

LOCKERBROOK PHOTO: TIM RUSSON

12 THIS IS LADYBOWER

Directions – This is Ladybower

↻ Turn **R** out of Fairholmes and take the second exit at the mini roundabout to descend past the wall of Derwent Dam. Follow the road up and bear **R** at the top – effectively **SA** – to ride along the eastern shore of Ladybower Reservoir. Cross the stream at the inlet of Mill Brook and tarmac turns to hardpack. Shortly afterwards look out for a bridleway through a gate branching steeply **L** up paving slabs through a field – take this.

2 Climb on the slabs – tough at the end into the courtyard. Bear **R** through the courtyard, cross a stream and continue climbing. Continue climbing through gates, eventually emerging at the bridleway that traverses the hillside below Derwent Edge. Turn **R** and traverse the hillside to the shoulder at Whinstone Lee Tor. Savour the view then chuck yourself down the great pedally descent to Cutthroat Bridge. After almost 2km, as the paths drops down and swings right towards the stream and main road, take the **R** fork to keep some height and traverse off across the moor with the power lines on your right. Moorland track leads to a gate – through this and the stream crossing. At a vague track junction after 100m keep **L** and plunge downhill to another gate. Through this and **SA** to drop down to the road by the Ladybower Inn (recommended).

3 Turn **R** from the pub on the main road to the traffic lights. Turn **L** at the junction and follow the cycle path on the right to the dam. Cross this – **please dismount** – and turn **L** at the far end. After 100m take the bridleway on the **R** –The Thornhill Trail – and follow this to the road. Turn **R** along the road into Thornhill. Turn **R** in the village by the phone box, following Carr Lane (signed *Unsuitable for Motor Vehicles*) to the village of Aston. Keep **SA** and at the brow of the second dip in the road turn **R** uphill signposted *Win Hill*.

4 Follow the lane, turning **L** at Edge Farm along the sunken lane, through two gates to emerge into a field. Cross this to a small gate and keep on the bridleway as it contours around, then up through another gate following a delightful rising trail onto the broad ridge of Win Hill. Keep **SA** to descend, on a multitude of singletracks, ruts and paths to eventually hit a gate. Keep **SA** up the rocky track, and then through another gate by the ancient Hope Cross. Keep **SA** up rutted track to gate – **SA** again – and cross the stream and through the gate at Blackley Clough. After a slight rise the track descends – great descent; very loose and stony. Join tarmac at the bottom and turn **R**, through a gate and descend then climb to the busy A57 Snake Pass.

5 **Cross busy A57 with care** and ride **SA** up farm track. Continue through gate past Rowlee Farm and zigzag up steep tarmac/gravel road that flattens off before reaching a gate. **SA** through the gate, continue to and through a second gate and on to a crossroads. Bear **L** – staying on main track – and keep **SA** on main track as it undulates down and then up past Lockerbrook Farm. Downhill through the pines for an exhilarating descent that spits you out at a gate by the shore of Derwent Reservoir. Through the gate and turn **R** to return to Fairholmes.

◄◯◯ Making a weekend of it
Cut Gate Special (page 87) also kicks off from Fairholmes and would be a good companion ride.

TOM FENTON DROPPING INTO COLDWELL CLOUGH

Introduction

This is a superb, challenging ride with a real 'wilderness' feel. Taking in some of the best and wildest scenery the Peak has to offer, this is a tough cookie that builds to a spectacular finale, crossing a 540m high shoulder of Kinder Scout and then descending Jacob's Ladder. The route can be ridden in either direction; described clockwise, this gives the very talented rider the chance of staying on their bike throughout – ride it anti-clockwise and you will be pushing your bike up the Ladder. Don't underestimate this ride; although it weighs in at a mere 23km, some sections are remote and cover some very demanding terrain – and right near the end it throws in one of the longest climbs in the Peak District! This route is rightly regarded as one of the classic rides in the UK.

The Ride

From Edale, a short road climb leads to a tricky climb up to Hollins Cross; this begins easily on grass but gets tough, especially in damp conditions, as the gradient kicks up. Stick with it – it's all rideable! Ride up and over Mam Tor for a quick adrenalin rush and hit the climb up Rushup Edge (spectacular views abound). Plummet down into Roych Clough and tackle the climb out the other side. Contour around Mount Famine to an exciting descent into Coldwell Clough and get ready for the big one – 300m of ascent, gruelling at first, easing slightly in the middle then rocky and technical at the end. You'll be well rewarded at the top, because the descent of Jacob's Ladder is a real plum prize – especially on a quiet day when you can have the trail almost to yourself. From here it's a pleasant cruise back to the car park.

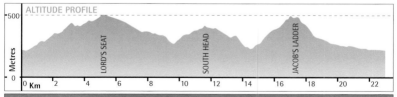

ALTITUDE PROFILE

LORD'S SEAT — SOUTH HEAD — JACOB'S LADDER

KINDER CIRCUIT   GRADE: △»▲

TOTAL DISTANCE: 23KM » **TOTAL ASCENT**: 920M » **TIME**: 3–4 HOURS » **START/FINISH**: EDALE MAIN CAR PARK
START GRID REF: SK 124853 » **SATNAV**: EDALE » **PUB**: CHESHIRE CHEESE, HOPE, TEL: 01433 620 381
CAFÉ: EDALE COTTAGE CAFÉ (VARIABLE OPENING TIMES), TEL: 01433 670 293

RUSHUP EDGE

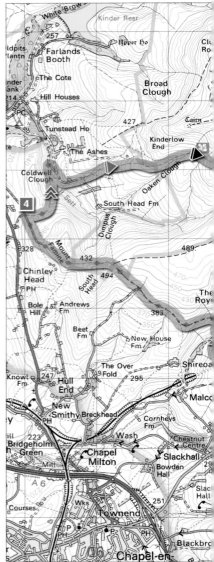

13 KINDER CIRCUIT

Directions – Kinder Circuit

↱ Turn **R** out of Edale car park onto the main road, towards Barber Booth. Pass works entrance and take the first **L** down a metalled track, cross a stream and climb steadily past Hardenclough Farm. Continue steeply up to a gate on the **L** (just before Greenlands). Through gate and **L** up pleasant gravel singletrack. Climb continues with increasing difficulty through two gates and with challenging sections up to Hollins Cross.

2 At the Hollins Cross viewpoint turn **R** up flagstones and through the gate towards Mam Tor. Continue climbing and bear **R** on path **R** of flagstones towards and over the shoulder (fence to your right), joining a short but exhilarating singletrack descent to a gate by a layby. Go through the gate and turn **L** up the road. Descend very slightly over the other side and look out for a gate on the **R**. Pass through the gate (signposted *Rushup Edge*) and begin a tough climb. Continue climbing, passing through a gate and up onto Rushup Edge. Continue **SA** along a vague level track through several gateways – always keeping the wall to your right – until the path swerves **R** through gate. Go through the gate and descend **L** to a fork in the path. Fork **L** here – effectively **SA** – and join a path through a gate at the bottom, adjacent to the main road. Turn **R** at a gate to join track that eventually descends into Roych Clough.

3 Drop down steadily to cross a stream then continue **SA** through a gate. Keep **SA**, cross another stream to a gate and go through this onto a walled track that culminates in rock steps dropping down to a ford at the base of Roych Clough. Climb steeply out of the clough, continue up the track to a gate and keep **SA** at gate to continue to climb less steeply. Ignore a bridleway to the left and keep **SA** up the track – now more steeply – up to a small col. Continue on this good track on a fast, flowing descent to a gate. Ride **SA** and then bear **R** down to a gate and onto a walled hardpack track. **SA**, smoothly downhill for 400m, looking out for a track, *Pennine Bridleway,* on the **R**, just before farm shacks (signposted *Via Kinder Valley to Edale*).

4 Turn **R** here and follow this track easily up through gates, after which descend with interest into Coldwell Clough. Hairpin **R** to drop and cross stream and follow the road as it curves left up the other side of the clough. At the end of the tarmac section fork **L** (more or less **SA**) onto a rocky track – a very tough climb! Keep **SA** through gates, with great determination, for 2km to gate at Edale Cross.

5 Track eventually flattens slightly before a short sharp climb takes you to the beginning of the Jacob's Ladder descent. This classic descent begins with a tricky section on steep steps. Continue with slightly less difficulty then take sharp **R** to a gate (ignore footpath on the left). **SA** on easier terrain before dropping steeply **L** into a loose, stony walled track with a gate at the bottom. Go through the gate, cross a footbridge – or ford if you are already soaked – and through a gate, Follow the track **SA** for 1.8km through several gates to Upper Booth. **SA** along tarmac road, eventually passing a parking spot and dropping beneath the railway viaduct into Barber Booth. Turn **L** along the road to return to Edale.

Making a weekend of it

If you fancy a Jacob's Ladder weekender, you could do this ride one day, and then the **Kinder Enduro** (page 103) the other day. You should be feeling it after that lot! Alternatively, there are plenty of other routes to go at in the Hope Valley.

GOOD KARMA IN THE BANK!

SECTION 3

Enduros

Warmed up? Enduros are rides that make the most of a day out in the hills. Make sure you've got your multi-tool, some lunch and a pair of willing legs. These are challenging rides for fit and experienced riders who want to feel the burn.

Enduros
sponsored by

Lumicycle
High Powered Cycle Lights

www.lumicycle.com

CHILLY RIDING UP ON MAM TOR, THE GREAT RIDGE BEYOND

14 Hope Valley Watershed

34.2km

Introduction

Commit yourself to this journey of discovery: this ride studies the life and landscape of the upper reaches of the Hope Valley, observed at close quarters. The interaction between industry, ancient and modern; agriculture; the flow of water – above and below ground; the mining past and the quarrying present; houses and barns, tourists and locals. All weave a web around the hills that make up the backdrop to the headwaters of the River Noe and its tributaries. The landscape is still evolving and what we see today, astride our bikes, is evidence of this changing history: farm lanes, grouse moor, ancient river valleys, canyons, packhorse routes, mines, quarry roads parish footpaths, Roman roads. This ride is long; there is a lot to see, height is hard won and the descents are sometimes challenging. Millions of years of geography and thousands of years of human civilisation, all coming together to give us one hell of a ride.

The Ride

From Hope, leave the world behind and track the River Noe into Edale along the broad shoulder of Win Hill and past Hope Cross. Drop down into Edale before soon climbing out once more to Hollins Cross and around the back of the bulkhead that is Mam Tor. Cross over into Limestone Country, keeping height above the very head of the Hope Valley above Castleton. Descend either Cave Dale – brilliant and technical in equal measure – or Dirklow Rake and Pin Dale, all very, very fast. Cycle under the Bladerunner-esque quarry machinery and into Bradwell. Once across the valley floor a stern climb and push onto Bradwell Edge gives access to the top of Over Dale. Traverse the head of Over Dale, to a great descent to Offerton Hall, before old farm lanes and ancient byways lead back through the hamlet of Shatton and the village of Brough to Hope.

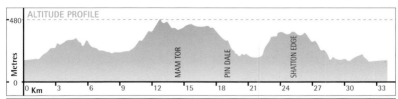

ALTITUDE PROFILE

480

Metres

0 Km   3   6   9   12   15   18   21   24   27   30   33

MAM TOR   PIN DALE   SHATTON EDGE

HOPE VALLEY WATERSHED

GRADE: ▲

TOTAL DISTANCE: 34.2KM » **TOTAL ASCENT**: 1,080M » **TIME**: 3–5 HOURS » **START/FINISH**: PAY AND DISPLAY CAR PARK, HOPE VILLAGE » **START GRID REF**: SK 171834 » **SATNAV**: S33 6RD » **PUB**: THE CHESHIRE CHEESE, EDALE ROAD, HOPE, TEL: 01433 620 381 » **CAFÉ**: WOODBINE CAFÉ & B&B, HOPE, TEL: 07778 113 882

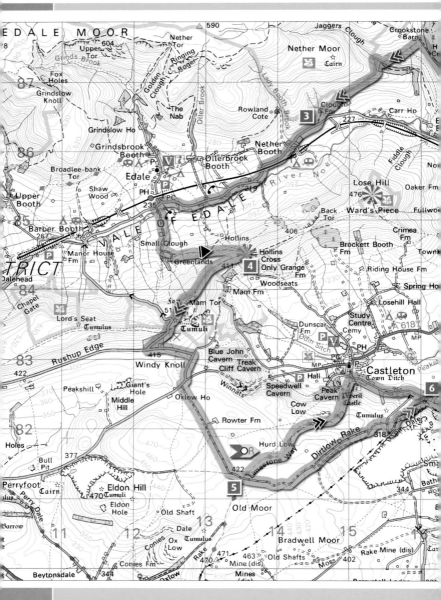

14 HOPE VALLEY WATERSHED

Directions – Hope Valley Watershed

↱ Turn **R** out of the car park and cruise east out of Hope. Take the first road on the **L** to Aston. Climb steadily uphill on tarmac and, at the top of the hill, take the **L** turn signed *Win Hill*, now on steeper tarmac. Follow this up to Edge farm and turn **L** onto the muddy, sunken lane. Pass through a gate, up to another gate, and keep **SA**. Follow the trail across the field to a smaller gate, contour around to the right, through another gate and then climb up the fine track to emerge on the broad ridge of Win Hill.

2 Turn **L** and blast downhill on an array of ruts and singletracks to meet a track merging from the left at a gate. Keep **SA** uphill through the gate and up to another gate at Hope Cross. Turn **L** signed *Edale*. Follow this downhill, through a gate, and on to a shallow ford at Jaggers Clough. Cross the stream, go through the gate and ride uphill on a good track. Go through a gate at the brow, spin downhill to and through another gate and then take the track and cross the stream, keeping the farmhouse on your left at the bottom. Follow the narrow trail down to the road.

3 Turn **R** and follow the Edale road for approx. 3km. 100m past the large pay and display car park and railway station on your right at Edale, turn **L** on tarmac to Hardenclough. Keep **SA** uphill as it steepens and, just before the road end, turn **L** onto the bridleway. Go through the gate and keep **SA** through another gate. The trail steepens, but remains magically rideable, up to the formal cairn of Hollins Cross. Have a breather and take in the view.

4 Turn **R** and head uphill through the gate and bump along the paving slabs. Go through another gate, looking out for tracks that fork off right but run parallel to the paving slabs – take these. The ruts soon give way to an excellent, swoopy trail making its way across the northern flank of Mam Tor. At the road turn **L**, uphill on tarmac a short distance. Once over the col, descend to the road junction and turn **L**. Following the road around in a big loop, looking out for a tarmac lane leading off **L**, signed *Rowter Farm Campsite* – take this. A word of caution: you have now crossed over from the dark side – the rough and charismatic gritstone of the Dark Peak, to the slick and slimy limestone of the White Peak – riders of a nervous disposition may wish to stop and change tyres, adjust suspension, or indeed swap bikes altogether. For the rest of us, keep **SA** along the track up to a gate at a dip in the track, and the meeting of several tracks. The sign – if it were not broken – would signal *Castleton* and possibly *Limestone Way*, down to the left. This is the infamous Cave Dale descent – our optional route*.

5 **(Pin Dale option.)** Keep **SA*** on the main track. The trail leads off, past several old, now-filled-in quarries, before a full-on rocky descent on the old quarry road of Dirtlow Rake. A full kilometre of fun! Meet the road, follow it downhill for 200m and turn **R** onto the track by a few trees, before the road descends too steeply. Follow the track for 100m, turn **L** down the shoot! Follow this trail downhill through the rocky chaos of Pin Dale Quarry. Keep **SA** to emerge at the road (Cave Dale option joins from the left).

*Optional Route – Cave Dale Option

OR Turn **L** through the gate and descend across a field signposted *Castleton*, bearing down and slightly **R** towards a small gate in a drystone wall (ignore 4WD tracks leading off up and ahead.) Go through the gate and follow the track down and **L** into Cave Dale, keeping the wall on your left to a gate. Go through the gate – track becomes very steep and very rocky (full-on trials skills required for success!), eventually easing as dale opens out. Continue **SA** to a gate. Go through another gate and turn **R** up the road to an acute fork. Fork **L** and ride slightly up and then down to a junction (Pin Dale option joins from the right).

LEAVING HOPE CROSS FOR EDALE

6 Turn **R** onto the bridleway, and then immediately **L** onto a fine trail that weaves through, under and around the infrastructure of one of the UK's biggest quarries. A steep tarmac singletrack turns into a track, bear **L** and head downhill to Bradwell village.

7 At the road, keep **SA** along Town Lane to emerge on the main valley bottom road (B6049). Turn **R**, through the traffic lights and take the lane on the **L**, just past the church. Follow this and turn **L** at the T-junction onto Bessie Lane. Fork **L** down into a dip, and then climb, forking **R** steeply uphill past the last house. Continue **SA** onto a path, to a gate. Pass through the gate and climb the often-muddy trail – very steep and basically a short carry/push to where the trail turns **L**. Variously-rideable, ascending singletrack leads up Bradwell Edge, eventually opening out and swinging rightwards to cross a grassy pasture, and onto a gate and a lane. Turn **R** uphill and follow the lane as it swings around leftwards above the head of Over Dale. Keep with the lane, **SA** at the track crossroads, and contour around and down to the large mast. Pass this and blast downhill to where the lane meets tarmac.

8 Follow the tarmac for approx. 10m and go **SA** through the gate (not the footpath gate, the medium-sized gate). Cross the short boggy stretch, **SA** across the field, and follow the now defined bridleway as it plunges down, fun all the way. Cross a small stream and pedal up to the gate and road. Turn **L** downhill past the houses, and keep **SA** descending the lane. Lane turns to track as it follows the valley back west, eventually turning back to tarmac at the village of Shatton.

9 Turn **L** up into the main village and keep **SA** to cross the ford (via the bridge in wet spells) and follow the lane gently uphill for 1km. Where the lane turns left up to Elmore Hill Farm, bear **R**, to and through a gate, and downhill through a couple more gates. Go **SA** on the tarmac lane to the road junction (B6049) and turn **R** to the traffic lights. Turn **L** at the lights and follow the main road for 1.5km back to Hope.

CLIMBING FROM HOLLINS CROSS TO MAM TOR

TOM FENTON ON THE DESCENT FROM MARGERY HILL INTO CRANBERRY CLOUGH

16 **Hathersage Circuit** – Hope Valley   29.8km

Introduction

An odd route, taking in lots of fast tracks, with fantastic views of high moorland and interesting valley landscapes. Circling the lower Hope Valley, this route is quick-going and rewarding, whatever the season. Some of the terrain will be familiar, like the superb ascent of Win Hill, and the notorious Beast descent to Ladybower, while some of the less familiar trails around Offerton will come as a pleasant surprise. A good warm-up for the tremendous Hope Valley Circuit from this book's companion guide *White Peak Mountain Biking*.

The Ride

Starting in Hathersage, height is easily won up towards Abney, before contouring around to Offerton Hall. From here, a superb moorland bridleway makes an easy ascent over Shatton Moor before a fast and furious descent to Brough. An ascent of Win Hill follows and then it's along the Roman road to the challenging Beast descent from Hope Cross. Fast hardpack is enjoyed along the shore of Ladybower, before dropping into Bamford village and then out again on deteriorating back lanes, to an interesting bridleway that drops back into Hathersage.

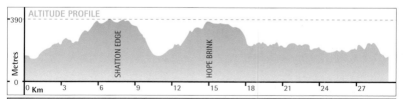

ALTITUDE PROFILE

390

Metres

0

0 Km   3   6   9   12   15   18   21   24   27

SHATTON EDGE

HOPE BRINK

HATHERSAGE CIRCUIT   **GRADE:** ▲

TOTAL DISTANCE: 29.8KM » **TOTAL ASCENT**: 1,020M » **TIME**: 3–4 HOURS » **START/FINISH**: HATHERSAGE PAY AND DISPLAY, ODDFELLOWS ROAD » **START GRID REF**: SK 231814 » **SATNAV**: S32 1BB » **PUB**: THE SCOTSMAN'S PACK, TEL: 01433 650 253 **CAFÉ**: OUTSIDE CAFÉ, TEL: 01433 651 936

OFFERTON MOOR ABOVE HATHERSAGE

16 HATHERSAGE CIRCUIT

➡ Turn **R** out of Hathersage car park and then **L** downhill on the B6001 towards Grindleford. After just over 1km turn **R** on a tarmac road signed *Gliding Club/Abney*. Climb up the road for 1.4km, branching **R** on the narrow tarmac road just before the farm complex of Highlow Hall on the brow. Follow the narrow road, through trees, traversing around the valley head, past Callow House. Just before Offerton Hall, at the right bend in the track, go **SA** on the bridleway across moorland. The track narrows and climbs steadily before a descent to a gate and a junction with road.

2 Turn **L** up the road and track past the mast and along a level rutted track onto Shatton Moor. At rough T-junction head **L** on bridleway, following track as it curves around **R**, passing footpath coming from the left. Pass roadhead on left and continue **SA** on an ever-steepening descent – excellent and rocky, becoming tarmac at bottom. Follow tarmac, curving **L** to reach main road in Brough.

3 Turn **R** on B6049 to the traffic lights. **L** at the lights and then first **R** up Parsons Lane to T-junction at Aston. Turn **L** through the village and after road dips, look out for sharp **R** turn uphill on tarmac (signposted *Win Hill and Hope Cross*). Turn **L** at Edge Farm and continue uphill to join muddy, walled bridleway. Climb track, eventually levelling off slightly and undulating beneath the south-west flank of Win Hill. At ridge, summit and junction with wide bridleway, descend **L** to join sandy track (Roman road) and follow this to gate. Pass through gate onto short climb to a second gate at Hope Cross.

4 Turn **R** here (signposted *Derwent via Hagg*) and descend slightly to gate. Pass through gate into rocky, sunken section and continue descent to next gate. Pass through this into the woods for a superb, rocky and technical descent (The Beast). At the bottom look out for a gate on the **R** – pause to drain out excess adrenalin! Head through gate and descend to south bank of Ladybower Reservoir. Cycle easily along track for 5km, finishing with easy climb up hardpack before track curves right and descends to dam. Cross dam **(cyclists please dismount)** and join the road (A6013).

5 Turn **R** on the road and descend into Bamford. In the centre of the village turn **L** just past The Anglers Rest pub. Go **SA** at the crossroads along Joan Lane (keep **R** at fork). Where the road turns right go **SA** on road unsuitable for motors – Hurstclough Lane. Ignore left fork at single bar gate to sewage works. **SA** to descend into Hurst Clough and get in low gear (you have been warned) for a shocking climb out. Continue **SA** on bridleway where lane turns left.

6 Follow bridleway **SA** through double gates to Nether Hurst, through the farm and **SA** through gate on bridleway descending to boggy stream. Cross the bog and go up the bridleway. Ignore lane on the right and keep to bridleway. Tackle pleasant, technical climb up narrow slabs, through gate and up singletrack to reach tarmac road. Turn **R** down the road to descend into Hathersage. Turn **L** at T-junction. **L** onto main road and immediately **R** on main road (to Grindleford). Turn **L** after 200m to return to car park.

A TAMER SECTION OF THE BEAST

CLIMBING ABOVE KINDER RESERVOIR ONTO MIDDLE MOOR

17 High Peak Circuit – West Peak

25.5km

Introduction

A good, demanding excursion into the western hills of the High Peak. Quite a varied ride, featuring killer climbs and equally killer moorland singletrack. Even though you're never really that far from civilisation, this ride can feel very wild and is tough on the legs – the mileage may not seem like much, but come prepared for a bit of an epic. Many a rider has started to fade long before the car is reached. Some of the climbs are big, but the descents are fun and the overall experience brilliant.

The Ride

From Hayfield, the riding warms up easily along the Sett Valley Trail – the course of an old railway. A little easy road-work follows, and then it's up onto the moors via a testing ascent over Chinley Churn to join a stretch of absorbing singletrack. After a hefty undulation down and up Coldwell Clough, the trail climbs steeply onto the western flank of Kinder Scout before making a fast descent towards Kinder Reservoir. Another steep climb – a feature of this route – is well worth the effort as we're deposited on the heavenly Middle Moor. Crossing this moorland trail – especially at the stream crossing – is perhaps the highlight of the route, but there's still plenty of good riding in store as the route loops through Rowarth and across the network of old rock-strewn tracks that lead eventually back into Hayfield.

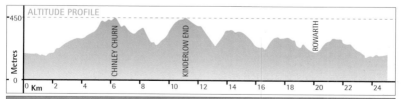

ALTITUDE PROFILE

Metres — 450 — 0

CHINLEY CHURN — KINDERLOW END — ROWARTH

0 Km 2 4 6 8 10 12 14 16 18 20 22 24

HIGH PEAK CIRCUIT GRADE: ▲

TOTAL DISTANCE: 25.5KM » TOTAL ASCENT: 975M » TIME: 2.5–4 HOURS » START/FINISH: HAYFIELD SETT VALLEY TRAIL CAR PARK » START GRID REF: SK 036869 » SATNAV: SK22 2ES » PUB: THE ROYAL HOTEL, TEL: 01663 742 721; KINDER LODGE, TEL: 01663 743 613 » CAFÉ: PLENTY OF CAFÉS IN HAYFIELD

MIDDLE MOOR

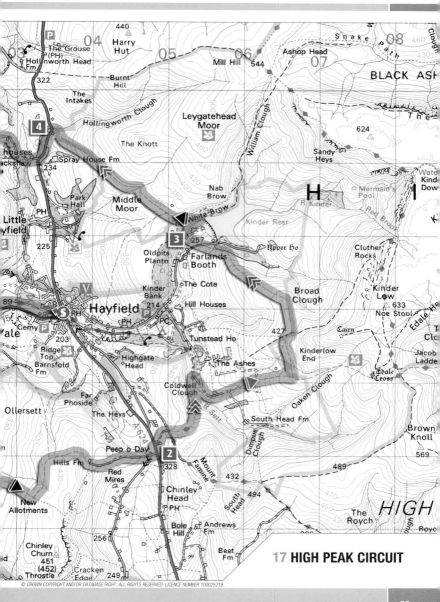

17 HIGH PEAK CIRCUIT

Directions – High Peak Circuit

❸ Head **L** out of the bottom of the Sett Valley Trail car park, pass through a gate and follow the very flat Sett Valley Trail for approx. 1.5km. After passing a large pond, continue to a junction with a road and turn **L** uphill to a junction with the A6015. Turn **R** towards New Mills and take the first road on the **L** after 300m. Climb tarmac, passing quarries on the left past Moor Lodge, and, as the surface deteriorates, continue uphill ignoring a track breaking off left to Piece Farm. The track levels to a junction – turn **L** on a bridleway marked by a fingerpost. Ride **SA** uphill through a gate and follow the walled bridleway out across the moors. Continue **SA** through two gates up a steep climb to reach a path junction and turn **L** onto a bridleway above the wall. Follow this for 600m to a path junction just past a gate and ride **SA**, not left and downhill, across the moor following the right-hand wall. Join a walled lane and continue through several gateways, making a steep descent to Hills Farm. **Please walk quietly through the garden** (as signed) and shut the gate, before making a fast descent on farm track to a junction with the A624.

2 Turn **L** onto the A624 and, after 100m, turn **R** onto a track just before a house and barn. Ride up the track past the old quarry to a junction with a gravel track – cross this more or less **SA** through a gate to join the Pennine Bridleway (signed *via Kinder Valley to Edale*). Follow this track easily up through gates, after which descend with interest into Coldwell Clough. Hairpin **R** and drop to cross stream and follow the road as it curves left up the other side of the clough. At the end of the tarmac section fork **L** (more or less **SA**) onto a rocky track – a very tough climb! Keep **SA** through gates, with great determination, for approx. 1km. Pass through a gate and **ignore** first (locked) gate on left, continue a few metres further uphill, looking out for second gate on **L** (signed *Bridle Path to Glossop*). Pass through gate and cross moor on sometimes boggy track, crossing a sandy footpath to join a wall coming up from the left. Continue **SA** keeping the wall on your left and look out for gate on the **L**. Pass through gate, continue on obvious path across fields and pass through open gateway. Descend, bearing **R** across fields, and bear **L** at stony track beside wood. Descend to metal gate. Cross road and keep **SA** down steep, walled path. Turn **R** at the bottom to a gate leading to a walled, cobbled path.

3 Pass through the gate onto the very steep walled and cobbled path (good effort if you clean it!). Turn sharp **L** at the first junction and continue the steep climb to pass through an open gateway. Turn **L** as the track levels out (right is footpath) to continue to a bridleway junction. Continue **SA** past the white shooting cabin over a wooden footbridge and then continue on fabulous singletrack and trail, past a stream, to make a fast descent to Glossop Road (A624).

4 Turn **L** downhill on the road and, after 600m, turn **R** onto Lanehead Road. Descend at first and then climb steeply on road passing the turn offs to Blackshaw Farm, Stet Barn Farm and Lanehead Farm. Continue **SA** where tarmac turns to hardpack and ride down past Matleymoor Farm. Turn **R** at the T-junction along the walled track, swinging **L** and downhill to the road (Note: this last section downhill is erroneously marked as a footpath on older OS maps). Turn **L** downhill to a house and large gateway: continue **SA** along walled track (bridleway), ford stream and climb to a gate. Turn **L** and descend into Rowarth.

5 At Rowarth village take first **L** by house (signposted *No Motor Vehicles Except for Access*), pass remains of telephone box, go through small gate with bridleway fingerpost and head towards white house, passing it on the right. Descend track passing more houses to join tarmac. Turn **L**, passing in front of The Little Mill Inn. After approx. 400m the road forks just before Long Lee; ignore the left fork and continue **SA**. Follow very steep, rocky track uphill. Gain flatter section of track and climb again more easily. Ignore a track joining from the left and make fast descent past farm to join the road. Turn **L** and, after 500m, turn **R** onto bridleway opposite cottages. Continue **SA** at first sharp bend left and descend steep, narrow, bumpy path to the road. Turn **L** onto the road, and then **L** again through a gate onto the Sett Valley Trail. Follow this back to the car park.

◄⊂⊃◯ Making a day of it

If you fancy giving yourself a good hiding, then link into the **Kinder Circuit** (page 69) in either direction from Coldwell Clough. That would be a big day out!

SKIRTING AROUND CHINLEY CHURN, MID CIRCUIT

18 Kinder Enduro

Introduction

Based on the traditional Kinder Circuit, ridden in reverse from that route, this ride extends out to the west, taking in the superb moorland trails of Broad Clough and Middle Moor. With more moorland, more hills and more distance it truly is an endurance test. A stop to admire the view from South Head will be essential for weary legs. The ride covers some big terrain, and riders will need to be well prepared and well equipped – escape routes don't really help here, it can be a long way back to the car.

The Ride

Starting from Barber Booth at the head of the Edale valley those unfamiliar with the area will find the wall of hills all but impenetrable, and the warm-up relatively brief. But, don't delay the inevitable: shoulder your bike and hike it up Jacob's Ladder. The keen/fit/tenacious will be able to ride big chunks of it (perhaps more with forks dropped and tyre pressures lowered) but alas clean ascents are few and far between. Once up we head across the high pass, marked by Edale Cross, before the superb descent down to and across the broad western slopes of Kinder Scout. Head up, across and down Middle Moor – ride it in August when the heather is in full bloom – and then around into the backwaters of the High Peak. The modest hills of Lantern Pike and Chinley Churn provide good sport both up and down, before that rite of passage – the traverse of Roych Clough – is encountered. The finale – the descent of the detiorating road of Chapel Gate – is testament to man versus nature, and losing height rapidly brings one wearily back to civilisation.

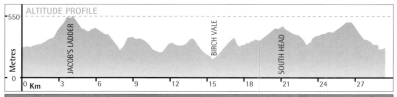

ALTITUDE PROFILE

550

Metres

JACOB'S LADDER

BIRCH VALE

SOUTH HEAD

0 Km   3   6   9   12   15   18   21   24   27

KINDER ENDURO   GRADE: ▲

TOTAL DISTANCE: 33KM » **TOTAL ASCENT**: 1,270M » **TIME**: 3–6 HOURS » **START/FINISH**: BARBER BOOTH CAR PARK, ADDITIONAL PARKING IN EDALE » **START GRID REF**: SK 107847 » **SATNAV**: S33 7ZL (NEAREST) » **PUB**: CAMELBAK FULL OF CHERRY BRANDY » **CAFÉ**: EDALE COTTAGE CAFÉ (VARIABLE OPENING TIMES), TEL: 01433 670 293

18 **KINDER ENDURO**

Directions – Kinder Enduro

❶ Turn **L** from the car park and follow the lane through a couple of gates to where it becomes track. Eventually go through another gate and across the packhorse bridge. Turn **L** and head up the rutted, walled bridleway: making the first corner is good, getting around it is very good. The track becomes a little more rideable before some final steep, steppy sections see comprehensive failure. Follow the track as it continues up, and down a little, to the col marked by Edale Cross.

2 Plunge downhill! Look out for a bridleway finger post on the **R** after approx 1.5km, just before a gate, and before the track goes down alongside a field. Pass through gate (signed *Bridle Path to Glossop*) and cross moor on sometimes boggy track, crossing a sandy footpath to join a wall coming up from the left. Continue **SA** keeping the wall on your left and look out for gate on the **L**. Pass through gate, continue on obvious path across fields and pass through open gateway. Descend, bearing **R** across fields, and bear **L** at stony track beside wood. Descend to metal gate. Cross road and keep **SA** down steep, walled path. Turn **R** at the bottom to a gate leading to a walled, cobbled path.

3 Pass through the gate onto the very steep walled and cobbled path (good effort if you clean it!). Turn sharp **L** at the first junction and continue the steep climb to pass through an open gateway. Turn **L** as the track levels out (right is footpath) to continue to a bridleway junction. Continue **SA** past the white shooting cabin over a wooden footbridge and then continue on fabulous singletrack and trail, past a stream, to make a fast descent to Glossop Road (A624).

4 Turn **L** downhill on the road and, after 600m, turn **R** onto Lanehead Road. Descend at first and then climb steeply on road passing the turn offs to Blackshaw Farm, Stet Barn Farm and Lanehead Farm. Continue **SA** where tarmac turns to hardpack and ride down past Matleymoor Farm. Turn **L** down the track to a gate at a junction of paths and follow the bridleway across the field, heading for a gate and track over the eastern shoulder of Lantern Pike, in the far corner.

5 Pass through the gate and follow the lane up, along and then down, joining very steep tarmac to the road. Ride essentially **SA** and descend a fine stretch of trail. Turn **L** at the road and ride up to the main road. Turn **R** and immediately **L** (effectively **SA**) up Morland Road. Follow this climb for just over 1km, eventually with a wall on your left. As the wall ends, bear **L** on singletrack trail with the wall (not straight ahead) and descend into the stream valley and woodland. Fork **R** and continue on good singletrack. The path becomes a little indistinct but fingerposts mark the way up to the road at Peep o Day.

6 Turn **L** and then **L** again onto the main road. After 100m turn **R** onto a track just before a house and barn. Ride up the track past the old quarry to a junction with a gravel track. Turn **R** and follow this track up past Mount Famine to the col at South Head. Great descending follows to Roych Clough, followed by not-so-great ascending to the road at Rushup Edge.

7 Turn **L**, staying on the path alongside the road. Pass through the gate and follow the lane up the rock steps – all very hard work but cleanable – to a junction of paths just after a gate. Turn **L** signed *To Edale via Barber Booth*. Pleasant moorland trail soon turns to a fast, loose and wonderfully messy descent – and plenty of it: this is the infamous Chapel Gate. Pass through gates, continuing along the main track all the way, and, at the road turn thankfully **L**, downhill. Turn **L** at Barber Booth to return to the car park. Good, wasn't it?

THE STEEP PULL OUT OF JAGGERS CLOUGH

19 **Mam Tor Classic** – Hope Valley

34km

Introduction

A superb excursion that makes the most of the riding across the complex of high ridges between Castleton and Ladybower. Avoiding any overly technical climbs, this is a fairly evenly-paced ride, within the limits of most mountain bikers and fully rideable even on first acquaintance – just keep focused on the loose steep ascent out of Jaggers Clough and relish the superb crossing of, and descent from, Blackley Clough.

For those familiar with the area, this ride makes a good base and one could pretty much extend and deviate from it to suit the day.

The Ride

From the tourist town of Castleton, an extraordinary crumpled sheet of collapsed tarmac climbs to the high pass of Mam Nick. Leaving this, we climb on quality singletrack onto the spectacular summit ridge of Mam Tor. A bumpety-bump descent leads to the viewpoint at Hollins Cross before the steady descent to Greenlands. Drop into Edale (brew stop) before an easily-won climb leads out again. Descend into, and climb steeply out of, Jaggers Clough, joining an old Roman road near the top and continuing through fine scenery to the superb, stony descent from Blackley Clough. Nip across the Snake Pass onto a steep but steady climb past Rowlee Farm, mainly on farm track, before joining the summit ridge over Bridge-end Pasture that leads us past Crook Hill and down to Ladybower. Cruise back to Castleton on back roads.

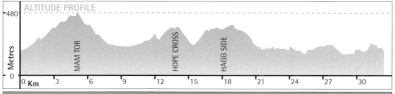

MAM TOR CLASSIC   GRADE: ▲»▲

TOTAL DISTANCE: 34KM » **TOTAL ASCENT**: 1,100M » **TIME**: 3-5 HOURS » **START/FINISH**: CASTLETON CAR PARK
START GRID REF: SK 149830 » **SATNAV**: S33 8WN » **PUB**: PLENTY TO CHOOSE FROM IN CASTLETON
CAFÉ: ROSE COTTAGE CAFÉ, TEL: 01433 620 472

DESCENT TO HOLLINS CROSS

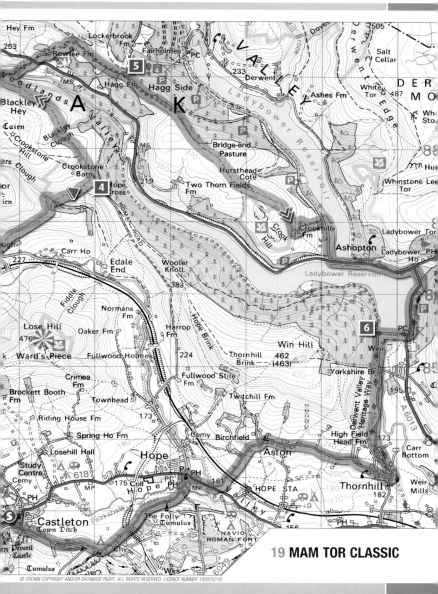

19 MAM TOR CLASSIC

Directions – Mam Tor Classic

➊ Turn **R** out of the main Castleton car park at the mini roundabout and follow the A6187 up the valley towards Mam Tor, ignoring the left fork uphill to Winnats Pass. Continue **SA** past Treak Cliff Cavern and **SA** again past the bus turning area. Climb up on steep tarmac through a gate and continue up the collapsing tarmac road to a gate at the top – watch out for drop offs! Continue along a short stretch of road to join the main road and turn **R**. Follow the road for 500m and turn **R** steeply uphill just past a parking area. Follow the road up and over the col – descend slightly, looking out for a gate on **R** by bus stop.

2 Pass through the gate onto the ascending path (left-hand path also drops to Greenlands at point 3 but is a trickier ride). Continue **SA** on singletrack over the shoulder of Mam Tor and descend to a gate. Through this and continue **SA** on stone flags through a second gate to four-way path junction (Hollins Cross). Drop **L** and bear **L** again. Good quality descent. Bear **L**, tricky at first with a few drop-offs. Continue **SA**. Fast, rutted and absorbing to a gate. **SA** to, and through, a second gate. Continue along smoother track to Greenlands.

3 Turn **R** out of gate near Greenlands, descending steeply on tarmac to road. Turn **R** along road, passing under railway bridge. After youth hostel and riding school, look out for a gate on the **L** – bridleway entrance (signed *Footpath and Bridleway to Alport*). Pass through gate and ride **SA** up walled path. Cross ford and through gate. **SA** up pleasant track through two gates. At second gate continue **SA** for steep descent into Jaggers Clough – get into low gear before ford and gate. Cross ford and **SA** up steep, loose track, which eases somewhat up to a gate. Through this and **SA** to a junction with the Roman road.

4 Turn **L** up stony track. Continue **SA** through a gate, eventually crossing stream at Blackley Clough. Through the gate here and, after a slight rise, the track descends. Great, sustained descent; loose and stony. Turn **R** onto tarmac lane at the bottom, through the gate and descend then climb to the busy A57 Snake Pass. **Cross A57 with care** and ride **SA** up farm track opposite. Continue through gate past Rowlee Farm, zigzag up steep tarmac/gravel road, which flattens off before reaching a gate. **SA** through gate, continue up to a second gate and go through this to meet a crossroads. Bear **R** on singletrack, keeping woods to your left, picking up main track. (**Do not** descend on track (to Hagg Farm) or continue around to left on main track, signed *Fairholmes*, past Lockerbrook.)

5 Continue **SA** with woods on left along singletrack across fairly flat ground to a gate. Through gate and continue **SA** as track becomes steeper to double gates, **SA** through gate, cross moorland (usually boggy), joining more definite path as it descends to gate. Through gate and **SA** across field, bearing **L** around the peculiar formation of Crook Hill's twin summits, joining more definite track down through Crookhill Farm – bear **L** through gates here – and onto steep tarmac track. Turn **R** at road junction at bottom to a junction with the A57. Turn **L** here onto cycle path. Follow this to the traffic lights. Turn **R** at the lights and continue along cycle path adjacent to A6103. At the dam, **dismount and cross** (please).

6 Turn **L** from the dam down a track (tarmac at first), looking out for a permitted bridleway after 250m on the **R** – Thornhill Trail. Continue **SA** on this disused railway through two gates to meet the road – head **R** uphill. On reaching the village of Thornhill, turn **R** just before the telephone box onto Carr Lane (signposted *Not Suitable for Motor Vehicles*). Ride steadily uphill through Aston. **SA** through the village and follow road as it bears **L** and descends steeply to drop beneath railway bridge to the A6187. Turn **R**, crossing the river into Hope (Alternative Start here). Turn **L** just before church and **L** at the T-junction. Cross the stream and head uphill to pass Hope Valley Cement Works on your left. Continue steadily uphill on quiet road before descending **SA** into Castleton at acute fork. Drop into the village and back to the car, or pub.

CLIMBING MAM TOR, ABOVE EDALE

THE FINE, PAVED DESCENT THROUGH STANAGE PLANTATION

20 Stanage Circuit – East Peak

Introduction

This is a route following trails that have become firm favourites with many Sheffield locals, easily linked into the city via the Sheffield Links midway through point 2 and near point 4. Describing a lazy figure-of-eight, this circuit incorporates a fair amount of road work, especially at the beginning, but the views are good and the rewards are great as downhill action is fully maximised and the best riding is left 'til last. The final, technical descent down through the Stanage Plantation is a rocky delight.

The Ride

Leave the car park below Stanage and gain height easily on tarmac, passing through picturesque terrain. Keep pedalling and enjoy the views as you swing by the Burbage Valley, drop slightly to Ringinglow and then head out across the ancient byways on Houndkirk Moor. A swift descent and another brief section on tarmac lead to one of the Peak's tighter bits of steep and technical singletrack down through Blacka Plantation. Climb back up to the Roman road across Houndkirk Moor before another leisurely road section weaves round to Redmires Reservoir. Leave the road and climb with increasing interest to Stanage Pole. Pause for a while – it's a great situation and the views west are expansive. A quick blast on a wide track leads to a choice of two contrasting, but equally good descents – narrow, steep and technical on flagstones, or wide and loose over rubble.

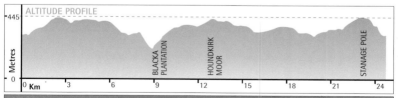

ALTITUDE PROFILE

Metres — 445 ... 0

0 Km 3 6 9 12 15 18 21 24

BLACKA PLANTATION — HOUNDKIRK MOOR — STANAGE POLE

STANAGE CIRCUIT

GRADE: ▲

TOTAL DISTANCE: 25KM » **TOTAL ASCENT**: 660M » **TIME**: 2–3 HOURS » **START/FINISH**: STANAGE PLANTATION CAR PARK
START GRID REF: SK 238838 » **SATNAV**: HATHERSAGE (NEAREST) » **PUB**: THE NORFOLK ARMS, RINGINGLOW,
TEL: 0114 230 2197 » **CAFÉ**: OUTSIDE CAFÉ, HATHERSAGE, TEL: 01433 651 936

ROCK AND/OR ROLL ON HOUNDKIRK

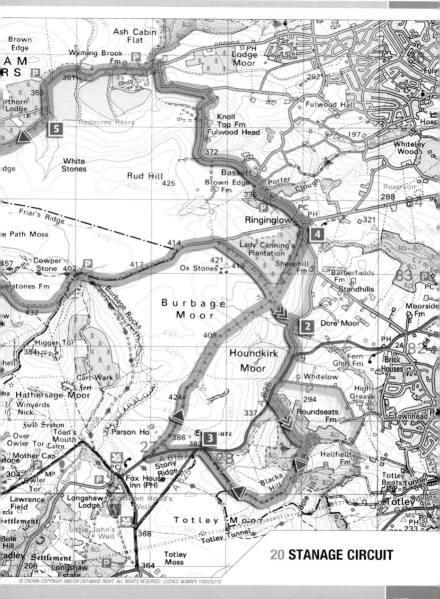

20 STANAGE CIRCUIT

Directions – Stanage Circuit

➊ Turn **L** out of Stanage Plantation car park and **L** at the T-junction after 200m to climb with Stanage Edge up to your left. Continue **SA** and turn **L** at the T-junction just after the large parking layby for Stanage. Continue uphill for 1.6km to the next junction and bear **L**. At the brow, bear **R** onto track to cut the corner through the Burbage Valley parking area and rejoin the road just before the bridge – turn **R**. Continue **SA** for just under 2km and look out for a gate and track (signed *Public Byway*) just above woodland on the **R**. Pass through the gate onto the track across the moor. Track climbs slightly before descending with interest to four-way junction – continue **SA** on fast descent to gate. Go through gate and turn **R** onto Sheephill Road.

2 Continue along Sheephill Road to a junction with the main road (A625). Turn **R** and ride uphill for 600m, looking out for a bridleway on the **L** (signposted *Public Bridleway*) that leads down through a gap in the wall and into the trees. This is the start of a fine descent; steep, narrow and technical. Towards the bottom, cross a wooden bridge and meet a wider path at the bottom. Turn **L** down this path and continue to a ford on the right (**SA** for Sheffield Links Return – page 180). Turn **R**, cross ford and begin challenging climb. Climb continues up steps, and then steepens to a junction near a bench. Head **R** and up, eventually meeting a gate. **SA** through gate, cross fields and bear **R** to join a track that leads to the A625.

3 Turn **L** onto the road (which becomes A6187), continue **SA** past prominent left turn and turn **R** onto a wide track on the left-hand bend (farm ahead). Head along track to a gate on the **R**. Pass through this onto Houndkirk byway. Track climbs and then undulates for 2.5km to the four-way junction passed through earlier. Continue **SA** past two gates to join Sheephill Road.

4 Turn **L** onto Sheephill Road and continue to a stepped junction next to the old toll house. Turn **L** and then immediately **R** to join Fulwood Lane. Ride **SA** for 1km, road dips slightly then rises past junction with Greenhouse Lane (junction with Sheffield Links Out – page 176). Continue **SA** along Fulwood Lane for 2.8km. Road drops steeply to a junction – turn **L** and follow the road as it curves right. Turn **L** at junction, drop down into dip past entrance to Wyming Brook and ride **SA** uphill. Continue past waterworks on your left and follow the road as it curves around the right-hand side of Redmires Reservoir, eventually turning to track.

5 At the end of the track, bear **R** to begin an interesting climb. Continue to and through a gate and continue **SA** to Stanage Pole. Bear **R** from here on a rough track for approx. 600m. From here there are two options for descent: the seasoned mountain biker will choose Option A every time as it's technical perfection. Option B is perhaps better on very busy days.

Option A – Stanage Plantation

⯈OP Keep a close look out for blue bridleway markers pointing **L** off the track. Cross the moor to the top of Stanage Edge and bear **R** for a few metres looking out for a stone flagged path leading down **L** – you need to cross a rock ledge and drop in somewhat to reach it – handle with care! Continue down flags with great interest to pass through a gate. Continue downhill to next gate – at least try to stay on the flags on this bit! Go through the gate and drop down a few steps. Do not bear right to car park (footpath), instead head **L** 50m from gate down a fast, indistinct path – watch out for a ditch just before the road. Turn **R** at the road and then **R** back into the Stanage Plantation car park.

Option B – Stanage Causeway

⯈OP From Stanage Pole bear **R** and continue to bear **R** following an increasingly rough track down the causeway. Bear **L** through a rocky section into loose stuff, which eventually becomes faster and a little smoother as you reach the parking area and road junction. Turn **L** onto the road and ride down then slightly up to return to the Stanage Plantation car park.

DESCENDING BLACKLEY CLOUGH, ALPORT MOOR IN THE DISTANCE

21 Hope Tour

Introduction

If anyone was in any doubt about the world-class quality of Peak District mountain biking then this route should banish such doubts. Over 30km of fully-rideable uphill and downhill action. Simply superb. Starting from Hope, this classy excursion, originally printed in the *White Peak* guide as a bonus route, describes a series of rider-friendly loops that take in some of the best terrain that the Peak has to offer.

The Ride

The popular turnpike at Hope Cross is accessed via a great little climb up from the Edale Road. Following the elevated course of the Roman road allows some classic Peak District scenery to be enjoyed, before the steep and loose descent that begins just past Blackley Clough. The riding that follows up past Rowlee Farm is stiff but not too drastic and soon leads past Lockerbrook Farm for a great descent to the banks of Derwent Reservoir. The climb up from here starts out earnestly enough, but stick with it – a concentrated effort will soon see you through the loose stuff before the gradient eases and the track eventually spills you back out onto that wonderful ridge that you just dropped down from. This time the descent is even better – a great rocky track leading to a series of quick bends down over the A57 onto the southern banks of Ladybower. An easy-going track, a great forest section and some cunningly-linked back roads then lead you (not without effort!) back up onto Win Hill for another fast and furious descent to the Edale Road and back into Hope.

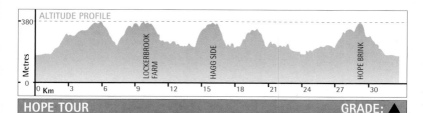

ALTITUDE PROFILE

Metres

380

0

0 Km 3 6 9 12 15 18 21 24 27 30

LOCKERBROOK FARM

HAGG SIDE

HOPE BRINK

HOPE TOUR   **GRADE:** ▲

TOTAL DISTANCE: 33.3KM » **TOTAL ASCENT**: 1,310M » **TIME**: 3.5–5 HOURS » **START/FINISH**: PAY AND DISPLAY CAR PARK, HOPE VILLAGE » **START GRID REF**: SK 171834 » **SATNAV**: S33 6RD » **PUB**: THE CHESHIRE CHEESE, EDALE ROAD, HOPE, TEL: 01433 620 381 » **CAFÉ**: WOODBINE CAFÉ & B&B, HOPE, TEL: 07778 113 882

CLIMBING HOPE BRINK

21 HOPE TOUR

➲ Turn **R** out of Hope car park, taking the first **L** onto Edale Road. Follow this, passing under concrete railway bridge and over River Noe on road bridge. Take first **R** – effectively **SA** – onto Fullwood Stile Lane just past bridge. Continue up tarmac track to gate. Continue **SA** through gate, track becomes stony and more technical. Follow this track as it undulates for approx. 1km (all good stuff). Continue **SA** where a sandy track comes down acutely from right, through gate, along the course of the Roman road, passing through a gate then up steep little section (choice of flags or singletrack) through next gate to junction at Hope Cross. Continue **SA**.

2 Continue past ford crossing at Blackley Clough, soon descending on loose and tricky ground. Turn **R** down metalled track, through gate and drop steeply, crossing river. Climb up to and **cross busy A57 with care**. Continue **SA** up farm track past Rowlee Farm, through gate and climb well-surfaced zigzags, eventually passing through a second gate and on to a four-way junction. Bear **L** on main track to Lockerbrook Farm.

3 Just past farm continue **SA** through gate. A short climb precedes a furious descent leading to a gate and the road around Derwent Reservoir. Turn **R**, following the road to Fairholmes. Continue **SA** at the mini roundabout at Fairholmes, passing two large (and some small) car parking areas on the right. Just past the second large parking area, a bridleway leads up and **R** through a gate, just before the cattlegrid. Steep at first, soon easing to climb through the forest.

4 Turn **R** at the top, through the gate to join a sandy track descending to the four-way junction passed earlier. This time, turn **L** through gate onto a steep stony track – a superb descent, one of the best in the Peak. Pass through two more gates and hit – not literally – the busy A57. **Approach and cross this hazardous road with care. SA** onto steep, stony and often greasy track leading down to bridge. Cross bridge and bear **L** up muddy track to gate. Turn **L** and down through gate onto southern bank of Ladybower Reservoir.

5 Follow the shore until a forestry track, signed *Bridleway*, heads steadily up **R**. **SA** at the crossroads where the track levels out. Excellent riding, mainly in descent, continues **SA** where the track tantalisingly drops down to a sharp, bermed left-hand bend. Follow level track back to join main shoreline track and bear **R** onto this. Follow banks of reservoir until a slight climb takes you up and away before turning south to rejoin the reservoir bank, passing the dam wall on left.

6 Continue down track, looking out for permitted bridleway after 250m on **R**. Turn onto this – Thornhill Trail. Continue **SA** through two gates to meet road and head **R** uphill. On reaching village of Thornhill, turn **R** just before telephone box onto Carr Lane (signposted *Not Suitable for Motor Vehicles*). Ride steadily uphill to Aston. Keep **SA** and at the brow of the second dip in the road turn **R** uphill, signposted *Win Hill*.

7 Follow the lane, turning **L** at Edge Farm along the sunken lane, through two gates to emerge into a field. Cross this to a small gate and keep on the bridleway as it contours around, then up through another gate following a delightful rising trail onto the broad ridge of Win Hill. Keep **SA** to descend, on a multitude of singletracks, ruts and paths to eventually hit a gate. **Don't go through it**, but hairpin **L** and retrace your outward route back to Hope.

◄💿 **Making a day of it**
If you were so inclined, you could link into the **Ladybower Lite** (page 11) from Fairholmes, rejoining our route at point 4.

LADYBOWER RESERVOIR PHOTO: JON BARTON

SECTION 4

Killers

They shouldn't actually kill you but they will certainly wear you out, building character in the process. Allow plenty of time, make sure you're well prepared and fuelled and then have it. Give it 100% and that's what you'll get back. These are big rides that reward hard work.

Killers
sponsored by

www.rab.uk.com

EVERY BOOK NEEDS A WATER SPLASH PHOTO! CRANBERRY CLOUGH

THE AMAZING CRANBERRY CLOUGH SWITCHBACKS

HIGH PEAK ESTATE
DOCTOR'S GATE

Welcome to the High Peak

This land is Open Country and you are free to explore - subject only to certain conditions (see bye-laws over) and occasional temporary closures for conservation management. We hope you enjoy your visit.

Sentinels of the Moors

The strange cackling call of the red grouse
the mournful wail of the golden plover
the bubbling cry of the curlew
these sounds symbolise the
wild mystery of the moors

If you are lucky you might see a merlin
dashing low over the heather
or a short eared owl floating
ghost-like in the mist

These birds inspired myths and legends in the past
Today they tell us how important
this fragile landscape is
for some of our most threatened wildlife

The National Trust is managing this habitat
so visitors can enjoy forever the sights
and sounds of this special place

Access Land

DOCTOR'S GATE – JUST REWARD AFTER THE SLOG UP THE A57

22 Bleaklow Circuit – Upper Derwent   64km

Introduction

Pedalling in a big loop around Bleaklow, this is the mother of all classics and an essential rite-of-passage for any (Dark) Peak District mountain biker. Although there are a lot of road miles, this route definitely shouldn't be underestimated – it's long, tough and tiring.

We recommend that you undertake it during the longer days of summer and set out properly equipped. Good dry trail conditions will make a difference, and a cool day again will help on those long, long ascents.

The Ride

From Fairholmes, scoot along the eastern bank of Ladybower before crossing the reservoir to a steep tarmac climb onto Crook Hill. Quality singletrack then leads along the ridge of Bridge-end Pasture to a fast descent past Rowlee Farm. After a few road miles on the Snake Pass, it's off out into the wilderness towards the truly wild, and potentially dangerous, plummet down Doctor's Gate. Skirting around Glossop, join the Trans Pennine Trail for some easily-won miles, which become slightly tougher near the Woodhead Pass, and head off once again in the wild for the ride's awesome finale – the classic singletrack of Cut Gate across the bleak Howden Moors. Attack the just-about-rideable climb up, swoop along the rolling top section and hold on for the balls-to-the-wall descent towards Derwent Reservoir. An easy spin leads back to the café at Fairholmes.

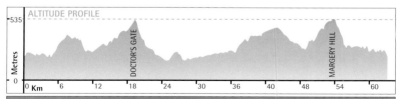

BLEAKLOW CIRCUIT   **GRADE:** ▲

TOTAL DISTANCE: 64KM » **TOTAL ASCENT**: 2,100M » **TIME**: 6–9 HOURS » **START/FINISH**: FAIRHOLMES
START GRID REF: SK 173893 » **SATNAV**: S33 0AQ (NEAREST) » **PUB**: LADYBOWER INN, TEL: 01433 651 241
CAFÉ: FAIRHOLMES VISITOR CENTRE, TEL: 01433 650 953

CONTINUES ON PAGE 135

22 BLEAKLOW CIRCUIT
– PART 1

CONTINUES ON PAGE 136

STARTS ON PAGE 133

22 BLEAKLOW CIRCUIT
– PART 2

22 BLEAKLOW CIRCUIT
– PART 3

CONTINUES ON PAGE 133

Directions – Bleaklow Circuit

➜ Head **R** out of Fairholmes car park, **R** at the mini roundabout and down below the impressive dam wall of Derwent Reservoir. The road curves round up **R** passing Jubilee Cottages and a telephone box. About 4km of tarmac and hardpack leads across Mill Brook to join the A57. Turn **R** onto cycle path across viaduct, then **R** again up road on western bank of reservoir. Look out for very steep tarmac road on **L** after 600m – take this and follow bridleway markers up and through Crookhill Farm, bearing **R** through two gates to the track up onto Crook Hill.

2 Follow right-hand wall (ignore all tracks that fork left). Through gate and follow wall for approx. 100m then bear **L** to cross exposed moorland – follow wooden marker posts towards gate. **SA** through gate and up through field (signposted *Bridleway to Rowlee Farm and Lockerbrook*) to gate. **SA** through gate onto easy riding following wooden stakes to another gate. **SA** through gate onto fast descent with woods on right to double gates. Ignore bridleway leading right and continue **SA** through gates. Follow interesting sand and gravel track for 1km to gate and junction with larger track. Follow track uphill to junction with good track. Turn **L** on good gravel farm track, leading down to steep, fast section with tight bends and then through gate past farm. Carefully join Snake Pass (A57).

3 Turn **R** onto busy and dangerous A57 and follow for 8km, passing the Snake Pass Inn after 4.75km. Look out for lay-by and National Trust sign on **R** side of road, 1km after emerging from woodland.

4 Turn **R** into layby and go **SA** through gate and follow track to cross ford. **SA** along paving flag track to four-way crossroads. **SA** to descend – through gate – on very rough track (Roman Road). Very technical at first, keep the river on your right. Continue **SA** down the track, which eases slightly but continues to throw in some very difficult sections. Approx. 3km from the crossroads, and after crossing the river twice, join a smooth, fast track to a gate. Go through the gate over the **R** bridge (ignore left-hand bridge which leads to farm).

5 After 1.3km and another gate, the track turns near some works into Shepley Street. Follow Shepley Street to T-junction. Turn **R** at T-junction and ride **SA** passing church on your left. Turn **L** along Wellgate/Church Street to fork and follow **R** fork to join Woodhead Road. Turn **R** along Woodhead Road for 500m to **L** turn into Cemetery Road. Continue past staggered junction and descend to Padfield Railway Station along Park Road. Bear **R**, then **R** again into car park and entrance to Longdendale Trail. Ride **SA** along flat, well surfaced trail for 7km, crossing B6105 at approx. 3.5km.

6 Leave the Trans Pennine Trail where the B6105 crosses the dam (Woodhead Reservoir) to join the very busy Woodhead Road (A628). Turn **R** and continue **SA** along A628 for 1.75km. Past point at which A6024 forks off left, cross Woodhead Bridge, looking out for **L** turn up track. Turn **L** (**ignore** steep concrete path leading left uphill) and go through gate next to small stone barn. **SA** up walled track, steady climb onto Pikenaze Moor, pass through gate onto undulating track, eventually rejoining A628.

7 **Cross A628 with care** and pass through small gap in crash barriers opposite. Descend grass track to cross narrow stone bridge over Salter's Brook and climb **SA** up steep grass track. Continue along track which curves **L** (N) across moor to meet A628 opposite road junction. Turn **R** along A628 for approx 2.1km and look out for a marked bridleway – The Snow Road. Bear **L** off the road and pass through a wooden 5-bar gate. Ride **SA** along rutted track, mainly in descent, to join A628 (again!). Turn **L** along A628 for 500m until just past Milton Lodge – look out for waymarked bridleway opposite beside Bord Hill Farm. Cross road and go through metal 5-bar gate. Descend slightly for 200m to a sharp **L** turn onto Swinden Lane, through the upper of two left-hand gates.

8 Follow walled lane slightly downhill through three gateways. At fourth, turn **L** down farm track to fork. Fork **L** on grassier track into Crookland Wood. Turn **R** after 400m, and ride **SA** down steep track to cross Brook House Bridge. **SA** up gravel track, which curves **R**, becoming quite steep and rocky. Continue up path onto open moorland and continue **SA** past steps. **Ignore** path veering left and continue **SA** past short descent to Haslingshaw Stream. Begin long climb up left-hand side of Mickleden Beck and continue **SA**, steadily uphill along Mickleden Edge (Cut Gate). **Ignore** left turn and fingerpost. This is just about rideable all of the way with determination and in good conditions (you are still fresh, right?). Path becomes upgraded and continues with interest to Howden Edge.

9 From large cairn at Howden Edge, begin great descent, first peaty and rutted, then onto fast flags, into dirt singletrack, into loose and stony path, finally dropping into Cranberry Clough. Look out for, and take, singletrack contouring off **L** before first steps and then look out for and follow blue bridleway marker pointing **L**. After steep drop into clough, and water splash, follow side of stream to join track coming in from the right. Bear **L** along track, through water splash, and continue **SA** as it rises above the river (**ignore** right turn to old packhorse bridge at Slippery Stones). Continue **SA** along well-surfaced track as it levels out and descends to join eastern bank of Howden Reservoir. Continue **SA** to join tarmac just after Derwent dam. Turn sharp **R** down tarmac and descend with dam wall on your right. Turn **L** at top back into Fairholmes car park – you've made it back!

DOCTOR'S GATE

ABOVE LADYBOWER ON DERWENT EDGE

23 **Killer Loop** – Hope Valley

60km

Introduction

If the area around Hope/Edale and Ladybower is the best riding in the Peak District, and the Peak District is the best riding in the Country, then this is the best killer route there is! While never remote, you'll see lots of people on this ride, plenty of other riders and you'll pass a few tempting ice cream vendors. This ride packs one punch after another, with the emphasis very much on downhill fun while trying to keep the climbs manageable. That said, the slog up past Gores Farm (Lockerbrook) towards the end of the ride will take some effort, but you're not on a Killer because you're someone who shies away from a challenge...

With seven significant climbs, and just about all the best descents in the area, linked by mile after mile of trail, the fit rider will coast back to the start, satisfied that this challenging route was well worth the effort.

The Ride

The ride is very long and very tough; the unprepared will find the constant ascending and descending mean. Tweaked since the first Dark Peak book, the ascent of Mam Tor gives a degree of gentle warm up before a brilliant descent into Edale. Back out of Edale and into Woodlands Valley, back out of Woodlands and into the Upper Derwent Valley – it keeps on coming. Out onto the Derwent Moors and back into the Upper Derwent, back out again and straight back down to Woodlands Valley. Around to the Hope Valley, up for one last view from the flank of Win Hill, and then the sting in the tail – the grunt up Pin Dale and the descent of Cave Dale – clean it after the preceding 59km and it's high fives all round!

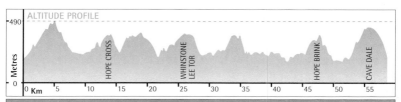

KILLER LOOP   **GRADE:** ▲

TOTAL DISTANCE: 60KM » **TOTAL ASCENT**: 2,300M » **TIME**: 5–6 HOURS » **START/FINISH**: CASTLETON CAR PARK
START GRID REF: SK 149830 » **SATNAV**: S33 8WN » **PUB**: PLENTY TO CHOOSE FROM IN CASTLETON
CAFÉ: ROSE COTTAGE CAFÉ, TEL: 01433 620 472

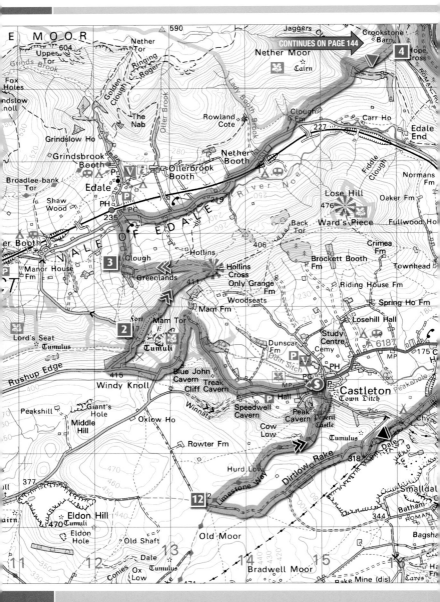

CONTINUES ON PAGE 144

CONTINUES ON PAGE 145

23 KILLER LOOP
– PART 1

DROPPING TO HOPE PHOTO: JON BARTON

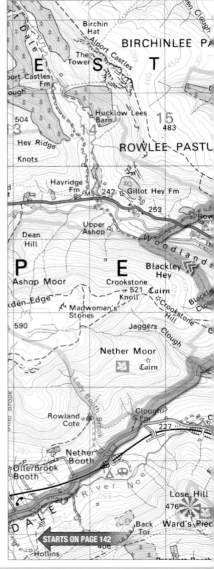

STARTS ON PAGE 142

CONTINUES ON PAGE 143

23 KILLER LOOP
– PART 2

Directions – Killer Loop

➊ Turn **R** out of the main Castleton car park at the mini roundabout and follow the A6187 up the valley towards Mam Tor, ignoring the left fork uphill to Winnats Pass. Continue **SA** past Treak Cliff Cavern and **SA** again past the bus turning area. Climb up on steep tarmac through a gate and continue up the collapsing tarmac road to a gate at the top – watch out for drop offs! Continue along a short stretch of road to join the main road and turn **R**. Follow the road for 500m and turn **R** steeply uphill just past a parking area. Follow the road up and over the col – descend slightly, looking out for a gate on **R** by bus stop.

2 Pass through the gate onto the ascending path (left-hand path also drops to Greenlands at point 3 but is a trickier ride). Continue **SA** on good singletrack over the shoulder of Mam Tor and descend to a gate. Through this and continue **SA** on stone flags through a second gate to four-way path junction (Hollins Cross). Drop **L** and bear **L** again. Good quality descent. Bear **L**, tricky at first with a few drop-offs. Continue **SA**. Fast, rutted and absorbing to a gate. **SA** to, and through, a second gate. Continue along smoother track to Greenlands.

3 Turn **R** out of gate near Greenlands, descending steeply on tarmac to road. Turn **R** along road, passing under railway bridge. After youth hostel and riding school, look out for a gate on the **L** – bridleway entrance (signed *Footpath and Bridleway to Alport*). Pass through gate and ride **SA** up walled path. Cross ford and through gate. **SA** up pleasant track through two gates. At second gate continue **SA** for steep descent into Jaggers Clough – get into low gear before ford and gate. Cross ford and **SA** up steep, loose track, which eases somewhat up to a gate. Through this and **SA** to a junction with the Roman road.

4 Turn **L** up stony track. Continue **SA** through a gate, eventually crossing stream at Blackley Clough. Through the gate here and, after a slight rise, the track descends. Great, sustained descent; loose and stony. Turn **R** onto tarmac lane at the bottom, through the gate and descend then climb to the busy A57 Snake Pass. **Cross A57 with care** and ride **SA** up farm track opposite. Continue through gate past Rowlee Farm, zigzag up steep tarmac/ gravel road, which flattens off before reaching a gate. **SA** through gate, continue up to a second gate and go through this to meet a crossroads. Bear **R** on singletrack, keeping woods to your left, picking up main track. (**Do not** descend on track (to Hagg Farm) or continue around to left on main track, signed *Fairholmes*, past Lockerbrook.)

5 Continue **SA** with woods on left along singletrack across fairly flat ground to a gate. Through gate and continue **SA** as track becomes steeper to double gates, **SA** through gate, cross moorland (usually boggy), joining more definite path as it descends to gate. Through gate and **SA** across field, bearing **L** around the peculiar formation of Crook Hill's twin summits, joining more definite track down through Crookhill Farm – bear **L** through gates here – and onto steep tarmac track. Turn **R** at road junction at bottom to a junction with the A57. Turn **L** here onto cycle path.

6 Cross bridge on cycle path and take first **L** up track, looking out for white gate on **R**. Bear **R** through gate past houses and head uphill on increasingly gravelly surface, through second gate. Follow track upwards, then down next to wall to meet T-junction with track coming up through gate on right. Bear **L** – effectively **SA** – uphill past gate, on tricky surface until fork in track. Bear **R** onto singletrack through trees to stream crossing. Cross stream, through gate and out across moor on good track to fork. Fork **L** and descend slightly as track curves left above Cutthroat Bridge.

7 Bear **L** onto wider track and brilliant ascent. After 1.5km join crossroads (good views from small bluff on left). Continue **SA** (signed *Bridleway*) on good, testing singletrack below Whinstone Lee Tor – wall to your left. After almost 1km turn **L** through gate to begin superb, rolling descent. Through gate, follow singletrack with wall on left. Through gate into steep rocky section, cross ford, through large gate to enter courtyard between two ancient barns. Look for small gate on **L** – through this and descend steep flagstones, bearing **R** at bottom to gate. Through gate and **R** – effectively **SA** – on hardpack track up eastern shore of Ladybower Reservoir. Cross Mill Brook and soon join tarmac. About 1.5km along this look out for telephone box and Jubilee Cottages. Just past this point follow tarmac road (not track), curving down **L** below wall of Derwent Dam and up the other side to Fairholmes.

8 (**Alternative Start** from Fairholmes.) At the Fairholmes mini roundabout turn **R**, up through the gates. Continue along western side of reservoir on tarmac for approx. 1.9km. After Gores Farm, road curves left round corner – look out for a gate and track leading up **L** into trees. Continue up track, which becomes very steep and slippery in all but the driest of conditions – a notable climb! Continue up lessening steepness, descend slightly past Lockerbrook Farm and cross stream. Go **SA** through gate onto easy climb for short distance up wide track. 400m after farm, track forks. Drop **L**, through gate, into superb descent (Hagg Farm) with bermed corners. Through gate – superb descent continues with loose and rocky sections – soon joining hard pack. Drop steeply, with care, to A57.

9 **Cross busy A57 with care**, through gate opposite and down steep and often slippery descent. Curve **R**, cross bridge and continue **L** and then up track – often muddy. Track forks at gate – go **L** through gate and descend to southern bank of Ladybower Reservoir. Cruise easily along track for 5km, finishing with easy climb up hardpack before track curves right and descends to dam.

10 100m after dam take the bridleway on the **R** – The Thornhill Trail – and follow this to the road. Turn **R** along the road into Thornhill. Turn **R** in the village by the phone box, following Carr Lane (signed *Unsuitable for Motor Vehicles*) to the village of Aston. Keep **SA** and at the brow of the second dip in the road turn **R** uphill signposted *Win Hill*. Follow the lane, turning **L** at Edge Farm along the sunken lane, through two gates to emerge into a field. Cross this to a small gate and keep on the bridleway as it contours around, then up through another gate following a delightful rising trail onto the broad ridge of Win Hill. Keep **SA** to descend, on a multitude of singletracks, ruts and paths to eventually hit a gate.

11 **Don't go through gate**, but hairpin **L** on wide track just before gate (almost doubling back) for long, fast swoop down the flank of Win Hill – not without interest and mainly in descent – eventually joining farm track at gate. Roll down track. Turn **L** along road, under bridge into Hope. Turn **L** just before church, **L** at T-junction, cross stream and head uphill to pass Hope Valley Cement Works on your **L**. Continue steadily uphill on quiet road. At right-hand bend, bear **L** – effectively **SA** – to climb steeply up a track past Pin Dale Quarry (motocross playground all around you here – some good drop-offs, jumps etc. to be had, but handle with care!). Turn **R** at the top and then turn **L** onto the road. Follow the road up past a left-hand bend and turn **R** onto the wide Dirtlow Rake track just before a cattle grid. Follow the track parallel to the road and then up and away from road. Ride **SA** along a track past a large quarry to your right and **SA** through a gate.

12 At a bridleway crossroads, take the track through a gate on the **R**. Follow this track across a field signposted *Castleton*, bearing down and slightly **R** towards a small gate in a drystone wall (ignore 4WD tracks leading off up and ahead.) Go through the gate and follow the track down and **L** into Cave Dale, keeping the wall on your left to a gate. Go through the gate – track becomes very steep and very rocky (full-on trials skills required for success!), eventually easing as dale opens out. Continue **SA** through two gates. Bear **L** down road to Castleton main road. **L** on main road back to car park. Phew!

START THE RIDE WITH WET FEET AT SLIPPERY STONES!

24 The Lord of the Loops

Introduction

Come and have a go if you think you're hard enough! The Lord of the Loops is designed for the athletic rider who has done everything and is seeking the next big challenge. Those of a nervous disposition should not look at the profile below.

Owing to limitations of space, we've supplied you with a sketch map for guidance only.

The Ride

The Lord of the Loops is big! Covering over 100km of gruelingly-hilly terrain, an early start, ideally mid-summer, should be deemed essential – and unless you're well fit already, you will need to train!

For those unfamiliar with the area, we suggest a few recce rides first, and good map reading skills are a must.

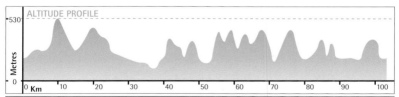

THE LORD OF THE LOOPS   **GRADE:** ▲»▲

TOTAL DISTANCE: 105KM+ » **TOTAL ASCENT**: 4,022M » **TIME**: A LONG DAY! » **START/FINISH**: FAIRHOLMES
SATNAV: SK 173893 » **START GRID REF**: S33 0AQ (NEAREST) » **PUB**: WAIT 'TIL THE END! – LADYBOWER INN,
TEL: 01433 651 241 » **CAFÉ**: FAIRHOLMES, CASTLETON & HAYFIELD

MARGERY HILL

628 Woodhead Pass

Trans-Pennine Trail

Woodhead

endale Trail

Langsett
Reservoir

HOWDEN MOORS

Snow R

Cut Gate

▲ BLEAKLOW

0 miles   1

Ⓝ

0 km   1

A57 Snake Pass

Derwent Reservoir

DERWENT
MOORS

SHEFFIELD ➡

⑤

Ladybower Reservoir

A57

KINDER
SCOUT ▲

BAMFORD
MOOR

EDALE

LOSE HILL ▲

WIN HILL ▲

A626

MAM TOR ▲

Hope

HOPE

BAMFORD Bamford

Castleton

Cave Dale

③

Dylow Rake

River

ELDON
HILL ▲

24 THE LORD OF THE
LOOPS

Directions – The Lord of the Loops

⟳ **Fairholmes – Hayfield**
Head past dam and cut **L** on the bridleway following the eastern edge of Derwent and Howden Reservoirs. Ascend slightly before dropping down to Slippery Stones (old packhorse bridge down and left). Continue **SA** out into open country, cross a ford then take path **R** up Cranberry Clough. After second ford the path climbs (**G.O.A.P.**) soon becoming rideable, but very challenging, all the way up to Howden Edge (pace yourself!). From here follow superb singletrack mainly in descent past a couple of right turns to footbridge at Crooklet Woods. Make short steep ascent to forest road. **SA** to **L** turn at four-way junction, continue **SA** to join Swinden Lane (track) and then bear **R** to join main road (A628). Follow this for 500m, looking out for bridleway on **R** – The Snow Road – just past the pub. This is awkward, rutted – a bit of an ordeal. Rejoin A628. Turn **L** onto bridleway that drops down to cross Salter's Brook, then climbs back up to re-cross A628 and join Trans Pennine Trail, eventually dropping down on gravelly switchbacks, crossing Woodhead Bridge, Crowden Reservoir and joining Longdendale Trail – a pleasing cruise all the way to Padfield. Use this as a chance to recover!

Follow Church Street then Newshaw Lane past church on right which leads through Brookfield and joins A57 into Glossop. Turn **R** up Simmondley Lane, towards Simmondley and then High Lane into Charlesworth. What follows is a long, long road climb that gains a lot of height but also packs in a fair amount of effort! Leave this road at Plainsteads farm, where minor roads lead mainly in descent to **L** turn onto bridleway leading to Matley Moor farm. Follow track **L** from here down to A624 (Glossop Road). Turn **L** and follow A624 for 500m, look out for bridleway on **R**. Interesting ascent leads across footbridge up onto Middle Moor where great singletrack leads past ford (tricky to climb out of!) and a second footbridge. Just past footbridge turn **R** (near shooting cabin). Pass through gate to join Snake Path and enjoy good descent into Hayfield.

2 **Hayfield – Castleton**
Pass church via wide passage on left-hand side, cross A624 to Sett Valley Trail Visitor Centre and follow Sett Valley Trail along course of old railway for approx 1.5km. When old factory is visible on right, turn **L** up track leading to A6015 in Birch Vale. Cross A6015, head steeply up tarmac road, surface soon becoming hardpack. Continue **SA** through gate joining rough track bridleway (signposted *Chinley via Chinley Churn*). Continue uphill across moorland, eventually reaching signposted junction. Turn **L**, descend slightly to gate, continue down more steeply through Hills Farm **(please**

dismount) and follow fast, farm track descent to A624. Turn **L** on A624 then **R** after 100m onto bridleway leading up past disused quarry. Turn **R** at junction (signposted *South Head*), follow track up then **SA** through double gates out onto flanks of Mount Famine. Well-situated track leads up to tricky section just before col below South Head. Continue **SA** to begin the much 'improved' descent into Roych Clough. Descend on track, through gate down into clough, cross ford then climb steeply (carry!) out again, following track **SA** up through a couple of gates, eventually reaching gate at A625.

Go through gate, turn **L**, then take first **R** down very steep road – exercise caution on this turbo-fast tarmac descent – there is a farm entrance very near the bottom! At bottom of hill turn **L** on B6061, head uphill (a bit of a grind), turning **R** just past quarry onto hardpack track leading uphill. Continue passing quarry on right, turn **R** through second gate across field to make descent to Old Dam. Turn **L** on road, take first **L** up Oxlow Rake, loose and stony eventually crossing field to four-way junction. Continue **SA**, bearing **R** across field and through small gate to descend Cave Dale. Approach the section as the dale narrows through a gate with **caution** – this is one of the trickiest descents in the Peak! Leaving Cave Dale through the small gate at the bottom, roll **L** down into Castleton – a good place for a break if you need one!

3 Castleton – Fairholmes

Join up with the A6187, follow this for approx 500m before bearing off **R** past Treak Cliff Cavern and heading up the old, collapsing road below Mam Tor. Follow this road soon reaching junction – turn **R**. Just past parking place, turn **R** again up steep road, crossing col then dropping a few metres to turn **R** through gate by bus stop. Follow singletrack up flanks of Mam Tor, then drop down at shoulder to join flags and descend to view point at Hollins Cross. Bear **L** and down from here – great value descent. Singletrack eventually leads to gate by Greenlands (house), head through gate onto gravelly tarmac, then **R** and down soon meeting road at T-junction. Turn **R** and follow road along Vale of Edale for 2.6km, passing below railway bridge, and look out for gate on **L** – bridleway entrance (signposted *Footpath and Bridleway to Alport*). Head through gate, **SA** up walled path, cross ford, through gate, **SA** up pleasant track for 1km through two gates. At second gate, drop down **SA** for steep descent into Jaggers Clough – get into low gear before ford and gate. Cross ford, **SA** up steep, loose track – thankfully track eases somewhat up to gate. Continue through gate, **SA** to junction with Roman Road – **L** here up stony track,

Directions – The Lord of the Loops continued...

continue **SA** to gate. **SA** through gate, eventually crossing ford at Blackley Clough. Pass through gate – after slight rise track descends. Great descent – very loose and stony – to join tarmac gate. Turn **R** through gate, follow steep descent on tarmac across stream, then up steeply to A57.

Cross busy and dangerous A57 **with care** and head **SA** up farm track. Continue through gate past Rowlee Farm, up steep tarmac/gravel road which flattens off before reaching gate. **SA** through gate, continue up to second gate, through this to meet four-way junction. Turn **R** through gate (**don't** continue on main track up to Lockerbrook). Descend steep, bermed track. Second gate leads into trees and stony descent continues to another gate, past which a short stretch of metalled track leads (**take care**) to busy A57. **Cross this busy road**, continuing **SA** down loose, stony, greasy track to bridge. Cross bridge and bear **L** up muddy track to gate. Turn **L** through gate, drop down to southern banks of Ladybower and follow this mellow track for about 5km – eventually climbing slightly away from the banks before heading south and dropping down to the dam wall. **Dismount** and cross the dam. Turn **L** and follow cycle path to traffic lights, join road and turn **R** up busy A57. Look out for Ladybower Inn shortly on the left – here comes the last big climb! Just past pub, turn **L** up double track which leads to gate. Turn **R** at gate, testing climb commences, soon levelling out onto moorland. Continue past ford and through gate crossing out onto open moor. At junction with track coming up from right – bear **L** and continue **SA** for some brilliant singletrack that climbs steadily up to col and junction of paths. **SA** here (signposted *bridleway*) to begin excellent descent. Track descends slightly (wall on left) before levelling off and taking a course through several awkward bomb holes. Look out for gate on **L**, turn through this gate and descend delightful roller coaster to second gate. Straightforward singletrack leads quickly down to another gate, where you enter a sunken track to negotiate a series of rocky steps before crossing ford. On entering courtyard surrounded by several ancient buildings, look out for small gate on **L**. Head through this and drop down flagstones descent through field to gate. Pass through gate and bear **R** onto track and continue north along shore of Ladybower Reservoir. Continue, crossing brook, to just past phone box on **L** where track forks and drops back down to Fairholmes.

Congratulations – you are a hero, you have our **respect**!

⚙️ **Making a day of it**
Just kidding...

THE CLIMB FROM CUTTHROAT BRIDGE

SECTION 5

A to B Rides

Two challenging rides that start out in the Peak and end up back in town – one heading east, one heading west. Use the train or get dropped off and get riding. Either way, there is something of a psychological advantage that comes with the knowledge that each pedal stroke is bringing you closer to home, the shower and a nice cup of tea.

A to B Rides
sponsored by

deuter
www.deutergb.co.uk

BLACKLEY CLOUGH (ROUTE 26)

CLIMBING OUT OF COLDWELL CLOUGH

25 **Edale to New Mills** – West Peak   17km

Introduction

A direct route across the highest pass in middle England, this ancient route is now accessible using modern mountain biking technology. Although relatively short and very direct, it is a challenging ride in the mountains. Obvious extensions abound, such as linking in with the High Peak Circuit (page 97), or following sections of the Marple ride (page 53).

The Ride

Leaving the isolated hamlet of Edale, a pleasant warm up leads to a hefty push up Jacob's Ladder to Edale Cross. This sets you up for the superb, fast descent into Coldwell Clough on the edge of Hayfield. Hard climbing then carries you over Chinley Churn, before more excellent riding lands you in New Mills. This is the most direct route, but armed with an OS map, there are many, many variations, extensions and, of course, return loops. The most obvious is to continue down the Goyt Way and catch the train home from Marple.

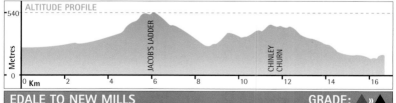

EDALE TO NEW MILLS   **GRADE:** ▲»▲

TOTAL DISTANCE: 17KM » **TOTAL ASCENT**: 680M » **TIME**: 2–3 HOURS » **START**: EDALE RAILWAY STATION
START GRID REF: SK 123853 » **START SATNAV**: NEW MILLS » **FINISH**: NEW MILLS CENTRAL RAILWAY STATION
FINISH GRID REF: SJ 997853 » **FINISH SATNAV**: NEW MILLS » **PUB**: THE RAMBLER, EDALE, TEL: 01433 670 268
CAFÉ: EDALE COTTAGE CAFÉ, TEL: 01433 670 293

Directions – Edale to New Mills

➊ Turn **R** out of Edale station, then **R** along lane, turning off **R** (signed *Upper Booth*). A pleasant tarmac warm-up leads to the farm at Upper Booth. Ride **SA** through farm buildings, through gates and along good track (Pennine Way) towards the steep climb of Jacob's Ladder. Stretches are rideable, but it's thought only a handful have cleaned the lot in one push. Bear **L** and **R** around the big hairpin part way up – cutting the corner straight on is footpath.

2 From the top of the Ladder continue **SA** passing Edale Cross. Continue through gates to the start of the superb long descent, rocky at first, then easing before gate. **SA** down field to gate. **SA** again, descending on good gravel track. Through gate and **SA** to join tarmac. Keep **SA** descending steep hill – at base fork **L** uphill on tarmac road for 200m to sharp **L** cutback on rough path. Make hard ascent out of Coldwell Clough, bearing **R** towards summit. Through gates, eventually dropping down to join good hardpack track at crossroads. Turn **R** and immediately **L** to descend to main road.

3 Turn **L** on main road and take first **R** on minor road after 100m. Bear **R** – effectively **SA** – through gate to climb up tarmac road. **SA** on tarmac bridleway towards Hills Farm. **Push bike** through farm and bear **R** through gate. Climb up narrow track to summit plateau of Chinley Churn and across moorland to gate and junction with bridleway. Bear **L** – effectively **SA** – on good, rutted, walled track. After 750m, as wall on right ends, turn **R** down bridleway to descend fast and furiously, through gates to walled track, following path/stream (!) to junction at head of Laneside Road.

4 Fast tarmac descent of Laneside Road to a junction with the main New Mills to Hayfield road (A6015). Turn **L** on road to the lights, **R** up Union Road, **L** at mini roundabout and then **L** to New Mills Central Station.

◄⊙⊙ Making a day of it

Plenty of options. This ride can be linked into the **High Peak Circuit** (page 97), **the Chinley & Rowarth** loop (page 49) and the **Marple** route (page 53) to name a few.

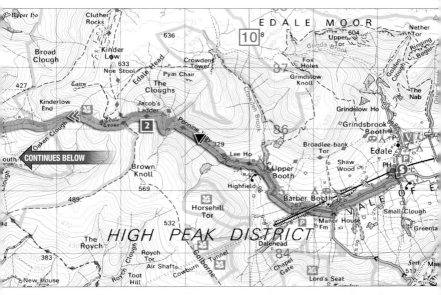

CONTINUES BELOW

STARTS ABOVE

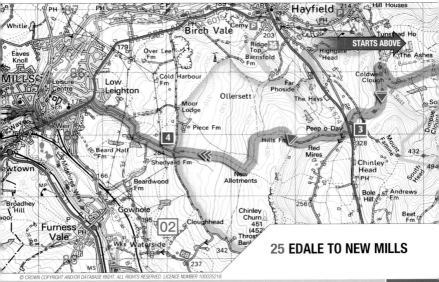

25 EDALE TO NEW MILLS

BLACKLEY CLOUGH

26 Hope to Sheffield – East Peak

26km+

Introduction

One of the great things about living in, or close to, Sheffield is the mass of mountain biking on your doorstep. Here's a route for a car-free day: take a train out, then ride back – of course you could get dropped off, but is that really in the spirit of things? This route is a reasonably tough challenge, but real heroes could throw in a few more loops to make a proper day of it – up around Ladybower, for example.

The Ride

From Hope Station, follow back roads to a bridleway up Win Hill. Quality singletrack along the ridge leads to a rocky descent from Blackley Clough to the A57. Easy tracks gain the height needed for the classic Hagg Farm descent before a mild cruise alongside Ladybower and a grind up the road below Bamford Edge (the views more than make up for the effort!). Catch your breath before tackling the climb up Stanage – few will clean it, especially at this stage in the ride. A fast descent to Redmires Reservoir leads to quiet lanes and a choice of descents into Sheffield.

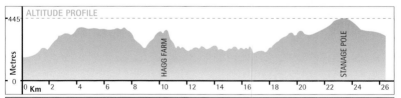

ALTITUDE PROFILE

445

Metres

HAGG FARM

STANAGE POLE

0 Km 2 4 6 8 10 12 14 16 18 20 22 24 26

HOPE TO SHEFFIELD

GRADE: ▲

TOTAL DISTANCE: 26KM TO WYMING BROOK » **TOTAL ASCENT**: 1,050M » **TIME**: 2–3 HOURS » **START**: HOPE RAILWAY STATION » **START GRID REF**: SK 181832 » **SATNAV**: HOPE (NEAREST) » **FINISH**: SHEFFIELD » **PUB**: NORFOLK ARMS, RINGINGLOW, TEL: 0114 230 2197; PLENTY MORE IN SHEFFIELD » **CAFÉ**: WOODBINE CAFÉ & B&B, HOPE, TEL: 07778 113 882

Directions – Hope to Sheffield

➎ Turn **L** out of railway station, follow minor road, through gate, past factory to T-junction – turn **L**. Cross railway bridge and continue **SA** uphill (Parsons Lane) to T-junction at Aston. Turn **L** through village, after road dips look out for sharp **R** turn uphill on tarmac (signposted *Win Hill*). Up this and turn **L** at Edge Farm uphill to join muddy, walled bridleway. Climb track, eventually levelling off slightly, undulating beneath the south-western flank of Win Hill. At ridge, summit and junction with wide bridleway, descend **L** to join sandy track (Roman road). Follow this to gate, through gate then short climb to second gate at Hope Cross.

2 **SA** up stony track, **SA** to gate, **SA** again to cross stream at Blackley Clough. Through awkward gate, after slight rise track descends. Great descent; very loose and stony. Turn **R** onto tarmac at bottom. Through gate and down then up to the busy Snake Pass (A57). **Cross busy A57 with care** and go **SA** up farm track opposite. Continue through gate past Rowlee Farm, zigzag up steep tarmac/gravel road which flattens off before reaching gate. **SA** through gate and continue up to second gate. Through this to meet crossroads. Drop **R**, through gate onto superb descent with bermed corners. Through gate as superb descent continues with loose and rocky sections. Soon join hardpack and drop steeply and with care to A57. **Cross (still) busy A57 with care.** Through gate opposite and down steep and often slippery descent. Curve **R**, cross bridge and continue **L** and then up track – often very muddy. Track forks at gate – go **L** through gate and descend to southern bank of Ladybower Reservoir. Follow the track around the shore, looking out for a bridleway (signed) heading **R** up into the woods. Take this, steep at first, before it levels off and finally descends once again to the shoreline. Bear **R** back onto wide track and follow this to the dam. Cross the dam (note sign asking cyclists to dismount). Join road and turn **R**.

3 After approx. 500m, turn **L** opposite telephone box up steep tarmac hill. Continue **SA** below crags and ignore track on right. Road steepens, drops slightly then steepens again before dropping to junction with road coming up from right. Turn **L**. Road curves **L** slightly to meet rough track coming down from crags at right angled corner, just after cattlegrid. Continue **SA** up this track, which soon curves right becoming a loose, rocky and technical climb. As track emerges through gap in crags it levels out – bear **L** along doubletrack towards Stanage Pole – good viewpoint. Follow rough track down and **L** of pole and through gate to make short fast descent to join tarmac at Redmires Reservoir.

4   Skirt around left side of reservoir, soon descending into hollow with car park on left.

Two options here for your return to Sheffield:

Optional Route

> OR for Hillsborough, Stannington, Crookes, Walkley, Broomhill etc:

5   **Wyming Brook:** Drop **L** into car park, pass through motorcycle barrier into woods and follow fast, rough track down to acute junction. Turn sharp **R** at junction and ride **SA** along track through motorcycle barrier to join tarmac road leading **L** along dam wall. Turn **R** at junction with A57 and continue to where road splits. Continue **SA** on A57 for Crookes, Walkley, Broomhill etc. Turn **L** onto A6101 for Hillsborough, Stannington etc. Keep your eyes open for bridleway options along either road.

Optional Route

> OR for Fulwood, Ranmoor, Hunters Bar, Nether Edge etc:

6   Continue slightly uphill past car park on to road junction and turn **R** onto Brown Hills Lane. Follow this as it bends left and continue **SA** to junction with Fulwood Lane – a steep hill. Turn **R** steeply up Fulwood Lane and follow this **SA**, passing a farm and then two turnings on left. Look out for Greenhouse Lane – junction with **Sheffield Links – Out Through the Parks** (page 176) and reverse this back into Sheffield through the parks. Or link up with **Stanage Circuit** (page 115) and return to Sheffield via Houndkirk Road and **Blacka Moor** – a good way to get over to Totley and Abbeydale, but a long day out.

SECTION

Bonus Section

*Now we come to the back of the book.
You've done all the rides in summer,
winter, day and night so what's left?
Here are what we think are the top ten
ups, downs and alongs in the area –
master these and award yourself
a massive pat on the back.*

*We've also compiled some useful
information for those of you riding
into or out of Sheffield, plus a bit
of info on Wharncliffe Woods.*

Bonus Section
sponsored by

RIDING OUT FROM SHEFFIELD INTO A PEAK WINTER WONDERLAND

27 **Sheffield Links** – Out Through the Parks   5.5km

Introduction

A useful way to ride from the city into the Stanage Circuit, or to link into the start of the Blacka Moor route and the awesome network of trails on Blacka and Totley Moor. The entrance to Endcliffe Park at Hunters Bar roundabout is a traditional meeting place for the city's mountain bikers, and this is where this link begins.

The Ride

A pleasant cruise of around 5.5km takes us through leafy parkland to the steep uphill at Porter Clough. Formerly a brilliant, loose climb it has been resurfaced by the City Council. Nevermind, as we emerge at the top we're spitting distance from the Peak and a choice of excellent trails.

Important Note: *Bridleways and footpaths often run parallel through the Parks. Please try to keep to the bridleways only.*

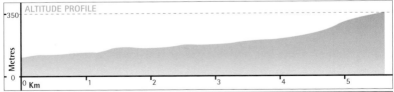

ALTITUDE PROFILE

Metres

0 Km   1   2   3   4   5

SHEFFIELD LINKS – OUT THROUGH THE PARKS   GRADE: ▲

TOTAL DISTANCE: 5.5KM » **TOTAL ASCENT**: 260M » **TIME**: 0.5 HOURS » **START**: ENDCLIFFE PARK, ADJACENT TO HUNTERS BAR ROUNDABOUT » **START GRID REF**: SK 332857 » **SATNAV**: S11 8PW » **FINISH**: FULWOOD LANE
FINISH GRID REF: SK 284842 » **PUB**: NORFOLK ARMS, TEL: 0114 230 2197 » **CAFÉ**: ENDCLIFFE PARK, TEL: 0114 221 1900; FORGE DAM, TEL: 0114 263 0751

Directions – Sheffield Links –
Out Through the Parks

⑤ From the Hunters Bar entrance to Endcliffe Park, head west on the A625 Ecclesall Road for 200m and turn **R** onto Rustlings Road. After 1km turn **L** at the mini-roundabout and continue into the park entrance on the **L**. Continue **SA** along marked cycle path.

2 Continue past The Shepherd Wheel on the right to meet Hangingwater Road. Cross the road and continue **SA** along the bridleway to meet Whiteley Wood Road. Cross the road, splash through the ford and continue **SA**. Upon meeting the next road, turn **L** and look out for a *bridleway* sign leading to a gate. Through this and up a short climb on a brick track. Continue **SA** along this to a road (Wood Cliffe). Cross this and continue **SA** to join a track. Bear **L** at junction after 300m and continue up rough track to Porter Clough climb. This eases and spits you out on tarmac (Harrop Lane). Ride **SA** to meet Fulwood Lane and **Stanage Circuit** midway through point 4 (page 115). Alternatively, turn **L** to Ringinglow Road and the start of the **Blacka Moor** route (page 5).

ABOVE SHEFFIELD, AFTER THE CLIMB UP PORTER CLOUGH

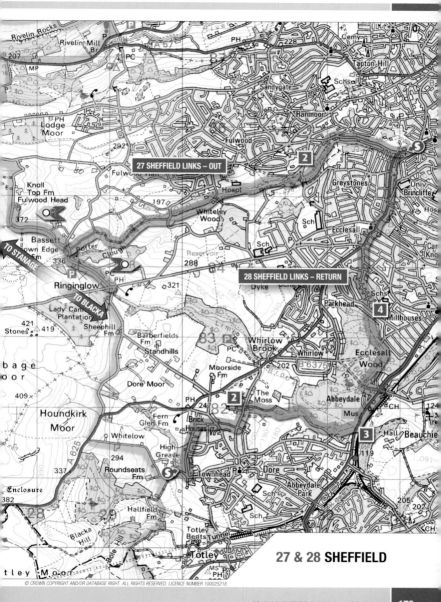

27 SHEFFIELD LINKS – OUT

28 SHEFFIELD LINKS – RETURN

TO STANAGE

TO BLACKA

27 & 28 **SHEFFIELD**

28 Sheffield Links – Ecclesall Woods 8.5km

Introduction

For those city dwellers living a little further south, the Peak can be accessed via trails in and around Ecclesall Woods. These trails also give a good return route into the city for anyone who has headed out through the parks – it's certainly better than spinning just on tarmac.

The Ride

Pleasant riding through woodland, particularly when the autumn turns the trees a mix of yellow and orange, and in the spring when the bluebells dominate. Not too technical, and popular with night riders. We've written the link up to/from Hunters Bar roundabout.

Important Note: *There are plenty of bridleways and footpaths running close together in the woods. Please try to keep to the bridleways only.*

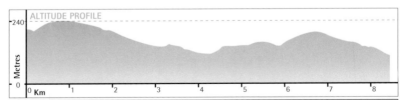

SHEFFIELD LINKS – ECCLESALL WOODS **GRADE:** ▲

TOTAL DISTANCE: 8.5KM » **TOTAL ASCENT**: 150M » **TIME**: 0.5 HOURS » **START**: SHORTS LANE, DORE
START GRID REF: SK 298811 » **SATNAV**: DORE » **FINISH**: ENDCLIFFE PARK, ADJACENT TO HUNTERS BAR ROUNDABOUT
FINISH GRID REF: SK 332857 » **OS MAP**: LANDRANGER 110 » **PUB**: PLENTY IN SHEFFIELD! » **CAFÉ**: WOODY'S, HUNTERS BAR,
TEL: 0114 267 6122

Directions – Sheffield Links –
Back Through Ecclesall Woods

➲ Turn **R** at the end of Shorts Lane (point 6 on Blacka Moor Circuit) to join Whitelow
Lane. This drops steeply and then climbs. At the top bear sharp **L** onto Newfield Lane.
Take the 4th **R** onto Kerwin Road, turn **L** at end and then almost immediately **R** into
Parkers Lane. Turn **L** at end of Parkers Lane, by the sports ground, into Limb Lane. Roll
down the hill, looking out for a signed bridleway on the **R** just past a dip (signposted
Abbeydale Road).

2 Turn **R** down this track. Ride **SA** through a gate and over a bridge. At the next gate turn
L over a bridge and immediately **R**. Follow the track looking for blue bridleway arrows
that indicate the track to Abbeydale Road.

3 Ride along Abbeydale Road to the crossroads – turn **L** here. Climb for a short distance
to a bridleway on the **R** (just past Abbey Croft). Follow the bridleway **SA**, cross Whirlowdale
Road, and continue following bridleway signs **SA**. Continue over 2 bridges; 20m after
the second bridge turn **R** between houses out onto Dobcroft Road.

4 Ride **SA** onto Silverdale Road and then Millhouses Lane (essentially the same road).
This meets Ecclesall Road at the top – turn **R** onto this and follow it towards the city
centre, eventually arriving back at Hunters Bar roundabout.

THIS REALLY IS WHARNCLIFFE ... HONEST!

Wharncliffe

A bit like the revered Fort William setup in Scotland, you could argue Wharncliffe too offers 'world-class' trails, as it's the training ground of bona fide MTB legend and Downhill World Champion Steve Peat. However, unlike Fort William, there's no lovely Gondola to get you to the top of the downhill runs here. Such is life. In reality, Wharncliffe is a big, steep, muddy, rocky forest that offers a bunch of technical downhill runs littered with drops, jumps and berms; a waymarked XC 'red' route; and a bunch of other hidden trails. One thing to note is that Wharncliffe does get muddy. Very muddy. So be sure to ride with an open mind, particularly if you're here in the depths of winter.

For information on the riding at Wharncliffe, and to download trail maps, visit:
www.wharncliffe.info

Note: *the runs here exist because of the Herculean efforts of local riders, particularly the Wharncliffe Riders Collective. If you do happen to ride at Wharncliffe and you'd like to help develop the trails we're sure they'd be delighted if you got in touch.*

Getting there

Wharncliffe woods are north of Sheffield, just off the A61. From the City Centre, drive north on the A61 for approx. 5 miles, passing the Hillsborough football stadium. At a traffic light crossroads in Grenoside, turn left onto Norfolk Hill, and then right after 400m onto Main Street. Drive through the village and up into the woods. Park in the obvious car park in a mini clearing on the left.

Grid Ref: **SK 325950**
Sat Nav: **Grenoside**
Facilities: **Car parking**

More information
www.wharncliffe.info
www.singletraction.org.uk

There are many killer climbs in the Dark Peak. Here are a few to test the mettle of even the most dedicated specialist. Only one rule that needs to be obeyed to make a claim – no dabs allowed.

Jacob's Ladder
GR SK 102853 – SK 077860

The mother of all climbs – included here more as a challenge to the mighty than anything else. The first section is loose and steep and has most folks off their bikes before the corner. The middle section relents somewhat and though rutted and tricky is rideable by most mortals. The last section past the rock steps, coming where it does, could well be the hardest section of technical climbing in the Dark Peak – is this the ultimate test?

Gores Heights to Lockerbrook
GR SK 166910 – SK 165896

OK, it looks fine on first acquaintance, but in the winter months this dark and dank uphill is slippery and often coated with decaying leaves. At any time of year the awkward rock steps appear at just the wrong time for a clean ascent. A formidable challenge.

Stanage Causeway
GR SK 227843 – SK 240843

The Roman road that makes a long, elegant curve up to Stanage Edge is a classic off-road climb. Never overly steep, the surface compensates for this by contriving to stay very loose, and by chucking in a series of tricky steps near the top.

Greenlands to Hollins Cross
GR SK 125844 – SK 136845

The first climb on our mega-challenging Kinder Circuit. It's becoming very rutty in the middle section and so a little harder than it was. A good effort, particularly on the final steps, will almost certainly guarantee applause from the weekend gatherings at Hollins Cross.

Chinley Churn
GR SK 021847 – SK 032844

The last 500m on the ascent to New Allotments are definitely clean-able, in the dry, if you're feeling strong! Hyperventilation guaranteed. (Photo above.)

Coldwell Clough to South Head
GR SK 050853 – SK 061846

Thanks to the work of the Pennine Bridleway team this is now just a plain old long endurance climb...

Brinks Road
GR SK 170853 – SK 168862

The climb out of Edale onto Hope Brink appears to be rather tricky on first viewing, but in reality it's a steady, almost pleasant, rocky lane.

Rushup Edge
GR SK 124834 – SK 112834

A challenging climb in a perfect situation. If you can master the start out of the gate at the bottom (steep, often very slippery, but OK in dry conditions), there's no reason that you'll not make it to the top without a foot-down. It's difficult to avoid being distracted by the superb views.

Jaggers Clough
GR SK 154872 – SK 159876

Start from the gate in the ford at the bottom of Jaggers Clough. Wet wheels do not help on the loose gravel steepness and it's essential to keep your front wheel down to avoid a buckeroo-esque dismount. Quite a short-lived climb but satisfying once mastered – the question is, can you do it every time?

Win Hill from Aston
GR SK 181843 – SK 172857

From the tiny village of Aston, there's a steep farm track that helps establish a good burn early on. From the top of this you enter a walled track that is usually damp with a muddy, loose surface – tricky to master on first acquaintance. If you make it to the top of this track you can relax as open singletrack rolls out across the side of Win Hill where the contours are easily gained right to the top.

top 10
Downhills

Graded on both quality and difficulty. It goes without saying that the utmost care should be taken on these downhills – ride with aptitude rather than attitude. This selection focuses on the technical, rocky descents that the Peak is famed for, rather than the swoopy high speed fun, we'll let you find those for yourself.

1 Cave Dale
GR SK 135812 – SK 150827

Starting out benignly enough, this limestone horror only reveals its true colours about two-thirds of the way down, just past a little gate. The intimidating, toothy, slippy rocky gully that is the only way down will make most riders keen to stay off the bike and start walking. Stay confident, keep the momentum going and go easy with that front brake – you might just survive!

2 Mam Tor to Greenlands
GR SK 125835 – SK 125844

From the gate on Cold Side (just below Mam Nick) a steep, stony shoot leads down to a second gate. The track past this becomes steep, rutted and twists alarmingly into a nightmare of off-camber ridges. Top tip – stick to your line choices.

3 The Beast of Hope Cross
GR SK 159876 – SK 163880

This great descent consists of three increasingly difficult sections divided by two gates. After a relatively steady start, at the second gate all hell breaks loose. It starts big and then the hairpins require real confidence and a positive approach. Keep your concentration in the closing stages – it stays loose right to the end.

4 Derwent Edge
GR SK 198884 – SK 187883

The descent from the track below Derwent Edge is a classic downhill experience – a real corker that is delightfully varied and only marred by the presence of three gates that briefly interrupt the force of gravity.

5 Stanage Plantation
GR SK 239844 – SK 238836

Difficult from the start, with a couple of drops leading to a tight hairpin. Brilliant flagstones follow, with a testing stream crossing and tight flags in the woods just to spice things up a bit. (Photo above.)

Brough Lane

GR SK 182805 – SK 183819

This steep limestone lane will have cobbles bouncing off your bottom bracket and downtube. A fall here will result in injury.

Gores Heights

GR SK 165896 – SK 166910

The descent proper starts around Lockerbrook. Straight away it's fast, with plenty of opportunities to catch air over the numerous drainage bars that criss-cross the track. Things then get pretty rocky as the descent drops into the woods and past a final hairpin.

Piper Lane – Blacka Moor

GR SK 282807 – SK 290807

A top descent, split into three contrasting sections; singletrack winds into techy rock drops, interrupted briefly by a gate (tip: don't go first – get someone to hold it open), and finally fast singletrack flies into the depths of Blacka Plantation.

Drop to Rowarth

GR SK 019885 – SK 014887

A real bone-shaker! This descent just gets better and better, characteristic of the real excitement to be found on the west side of the Peak.

Hollins Cross to Greenlands

GR SK 136845 – SK 125844

Is this a top-ten downhill? We think it just qualifies thanks to the steep, technical, rock-step introduction that sets the pace right from the start. Increasingly smooth and flowing as the steepness relents, don't get caught out by the deep ruts and adverse cambers that keep things interesting throughout.

top 10 Singletrack

Dark Peak singletrack has its own, unique character – short and sharp, offering concentrated technical value. Littered with ruts, bomb holes and rocky sections – often in glorious high moorland settings – this selection is guaranteed to leave a lasting impression on any serious mountain biker.

1 Howden Edge to Slippery Stones (Cut Gate)   GR SK 183958 – SK 169952

The section of descent from the col at Howden Edge is a singletrack classic. Beginning steep and rutted, a thin strip of dirt then breaks out across the open moor. Things soon become narrow, stony and loose past a couple of hairpins to the rock steps. Don't miss the signposted left turn on this last section – you will be approaching it fast and there's still a great little hairpin to come. Very satisfying!

2 Derwent Edge to Cutthroat Bridge   GR SK 198873 – SK 213874

In dry conditions this becomes a textbook ribbon of silvery-grey, gritty sand. Quite wide now, and unfortunately getting wider, 'ethical riding' makes this a real blast in descent.

3 Cut Gate to North America   GR SK 191985 – SK 203997

Not overly long, but very scenic, this great little portion of moorland can be as tricky as you want to make it (take care with your line choices!). A superb variety of surfaces and some great opportunities to grab air make this lovely section of singletrack a real winner.

4 Bradwell Edge   GR SK 182810 – SK 178806

The singletrack drop off Bradwell Edge is wonderfully steep and tight in places, and best enjoyed in the summer months.

5 Middle Moor   GR SK 049883 – SK 035894

A really peachy section of rolling, moorland trail. The only real interruption to this fast and flowing feast is the ford about a third of the way along – but even this should be style-able with a bit of luck and cunning use of gears.

Win Hill

GR SK 179845 – SK 172857

OK it's mostly a climb, but the much-photographed singletrack section up the southern flank of Win Hill is an essential rite of passage for any Peak mountain biker – and the views just keep getting better and better.

Chinley Churn

GR Loads!

This oddly-named and seldom-visited western outpost of the Dark Peak is criss-crossed by loads of great quality singletrack – all full of character. Best in the dry, this is a great little hill to explore at leisure.

Shatton Edge to Offerton Hall

GR SK 200814 – SK 212810

Good solid descending fun, much of it on narrow singletrack.

Wimble Holme Hill

GR SK 290796 – SK 286797

A very short section of singletrack that's included here because it comes with an almost unique penalty for failure – on the right hand side is a steep, rocky drop into the bilberrys. Actually quite a test of nerve and balance, it's livened up by a couple of black squelchy bog holes – obviously designed by nature's great trailbuilder to catch out the unwary! (Photo above.)

Wharncliffe

GR SK 325949 (car park)

At their best in the drier months, the woods at Wharncliffe are littered with quality singletrack. The Wharncliffe Riders Collective continue their hard work to build and maintain trails in the woods and you can't really knock the superb work that has been done here. Get involved: **www.wharncliffe.info**

Appendix

Tourist Information Centres

www.visitpeakdistrict.com – Official tourism
website for the Peak District & Derbyshire
www.peakdistrict.org – Official website of the
Peak District National Park Authority

Castleton . . . . T: 01433 816 572
Edale . . . . T: 01433 670 207
Glossop. . . . . T: 01457 855 920
Ladybower (Fairholmes) . . . . . T: 01433 650 953
Sheffield. . . . . T: 0114 221 1900

Bike Shops

18Bikes, Hope . . . . T: 01433 621 111
High Peak Cycles, Glossop . . . T: 01457 861 535
Sett Valley Cycles, New Mills.. T: 01633 742 629
J E James, Sheffield . . . . T: 0114 292 3102
J E James, Chesterfield . . . . . . T: 01246 453 453
Langsett Cycles, Sheffield. . . . T: 0114 234 8191
Bike Factory, Whaley Bridge . . T: 01663 735 020

Outdoor Shops

Not bike shops, but useful for maps, clothing,
energy bars etc.

Outside, Hathersage . . . . T: 01433 651 936
The Square, Hathersage . . . . . T: 01433 698 109
CCC, Hathersage . . . . T: 01433 659 870
Hitch n Hike, Hope . . . . T: 01433 623 331
Hitch n Hike, Bamford. . . . . . . T: 01433 651 013
Castleton – loads!

Bike Hire

Forgotten your bike?

18Bikes – Demo ace rides from
Cotic, Pace, Santa Cruz etc . . T: 01433 621 111
Derwent Cycle Hire,
Fairholmes, Ladybower . . . . . . T: 01433 651 261

Food and Drink
Cafés

The Peak District is fully geared up for mid- and
post-ride refuelling sessions. Cafés vary from the
distinctly twee to the greasiest spoon. Here's a
selection recommended by the team:

Woodbine Café, Hope . . . . T: 07778 113 882
Log fire; very warm welcome – even for the muddiest.
Nice coffee and large portions of home-made pie.
Also does B&B.
Edale Cottage Café, Edale. . . . T: 01433 670 293
Basic, but good value café serving greasy spoon
fare to all. Variable opening times.
Outside Café, Hathersage . . . . T: 01433 651 936
Upstairs, above the Outside shop in Hathersage.
Popular with climbers, walkers and road cyclists.
Good selection of cakes and snacks.
Three Roofs Café,
Castleton . . . . T: 01433 620 533
Variable opening times. Don't muddy the doilies.
Bank View Café, Langsett. . . . T: 01226 762 337
Can prove elusive! Roughly opposite the Waggon and
Horses pub on the main road. Variable opening times.

Pubs

There are lots of good pubs in the Peak District –
all well worthy of a visit for post- or mid-ride
refreshment. Here's a selection that can be
accessed from the routes in this guide.

The Norfolk Arms,
Ringinglow . . . . T: 0114 230 2197
The Fox House Inn,
Longshaw. . . . . .T: 0845 11 26 041
The Ladybower Inn, Bamford . . T: 01433 651 241
The Cheshire Cheese Inn,
Hope . . . . T: 01433 620 381
The Travellers Rest, Brough . . T: 01433 620 363
The Waltzing Weasel Inn,
Birch Vale . . . . T: 01663 743 402
The Royal Hotel, Hayfield. . . . T: 01633 742 721

Weather

www.bbc.co.uk/weather
www.metoffice.com

Accommodation
YHA

Castleton .... T: 0845 371 9628
Edale .... T: 0845 371 9514
Hathersage .... T: 0845 371 9021

Hotels, Self Catering & B&B

It's beyond the remit of this guide to give a full list of accommodation in the Peak. Here are a few we would recommend, but your best bet is to contact the nearest T.I.C. to your planned ride.

Woodbine Café and B&B .... T: 07778 113 882
Round Meadow Barn, Hope .. T: 01433 621 347
The Woodroffe Arms, Hope .. T: 01433 620 351
The Cheshire Cheese Inn,
Hope .... T: 01433 620 381
The Waltzing Weasel Inn,
Birch Vale .... T: 01663 743 402

Camping

There are a few campsites in the Hope Valley.

North Lees, Hathersage ...... T: 01433 650 838

Other Publications

White Peak Mountain Biking – The Pure Trails
Jon Barton, Vertebrate Publishing
www.v-publishing.co.uk

Cycling in the Peak District: Off-Road Trails & Quiet Lanes
Tom Fenton & Jon Barton, Vertebrate Publishing
www.v-publishing.co.uk

Mountain Biking Trail Centres – The Guide
Tom Fenton, Vertebrate Publishing
www.v-publishing.co.uk

About the Author

Jon lives in the heart of the Peak District, with his wife, young son and novelty show dog (Wilbur). Having ridden and climbed in the area for over 15 years his knowledge of the Peak, and particularly the Hope Valley, is enviable. After the shackles of fame that came with authoring the original Dark Peak Mountain Biking guidebook, Jon had to improve his MTB skills somewhat. Now proficient at singletrack, and merely nervous of descents, his ambition *still* remains to clean the climb up Gores Heights (Lockerbrook). Catch him there most weekends for book signings. Don't be put off by the blue language, or his disproportionately large calves, he's really approachable and surprisingly down to earth.

About the Photographer

As well as being Vertebrate's Publishing Manager and chief tormentor of his boss, John Coefield is also an accomplished photographer with images regularly published in a variety of national publications, including Climb Magazine, Climber Magazine and numerous rock climbing guidebooks. John has been riding since a young age and these days divides his time almost equally between riding, rock climbing, photography and his young family. To view more of John's images visit: **www.johncoefield.com**

Vertebrate Publishing

Mountain Bike Rider (MBR) Magazine called our MTB guides *"...a series of glossy, highly polished and well researched guidebooks to some of the UK's favourite riding spots."*

That's our plan, and we're almost there. We want to provide you – the rider – with well-researched, informative, functional, inspirational and great-looking MTB guidebooks that document the superb riding across the length and breadth of the UK. So if you want to go riding somewhere, you can count on us to point you in the right direction.

We're one of a new breed of independent publishers, dedicated to producing the very best outdoor leisure titles. As well as our series of MTB guidebooks, we have critically acclaimed and bestselling titles covering a range of leisure activities, including; cycling, rock climbing, hillwalking and others. We are best known for our MTB titles, including the original **Dark Peak Mountain Biking**, which BIKEmagic.com said was *"far and away the best Peak guide we've come across"*. Our autobiography of rock climber Jerry Moffatt won the Grand Prize at the 2009 Banff Mountain Book Festival.

We also produce many leading outdoor titles for other publishers including the **Mountain Leader** and **Walking Group Leader Schemes** (MLTUK) and rock climbing guidebooks for the **British Mountaineering Council** and the **Fell and Rock Climbing Club**. For more information, please visit our website: **www.v-publishing.co.uk** or email us: **info@v-publishing.co.uk**

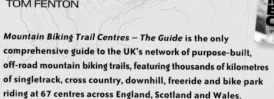

VERTEBRATE PUBLISHING

MOUNTAIN BIKING GUIDEBOOKS

About the Great Outdoors

The great outdoors is not bottom bracket friendly; beautiful flowing singletrack can give way suddenly to scary rock gardens, hard climbs can appear right at the end of a ride and sheep will laugh at your attempts to clean your nemesis descent. Of course it's not all good news. You'll need a good bike to ride many of the routes in our set of mountain biking guides. You'll also need fuel, spare clothing, first aid skills, endurance, power, determination and plenty of nerve.

Bridleways litter our great outdoors. Our guides, written by local riders, reveal the secrets of their local area's best rides from 6 to 300km in length, including ideas for link-ups and night-riding options. Critically acclaimed, our comprehensive series of guides is the country's bestselling and most respected – purpose-built for the modern mountain biker.

The Guidebooks

Each guidebook features up to 28 rides, complete with comprehensive directions, specialist mapping and inspiring photography, all in a pocket-sized, portable format. Written by riders for riders, our guides are designed to maximise ride-ability and are full of useful local area information.